THE
ENDS
OF
KINGS

An illustrated guide to the death and burial places of English monarchs

Geoff Brown

AMBERLEY

For Alice, with love

Front cover: Detail from the tomb of Edward II. With kind permission of Gloucester Cathedral Dean and Chapter. Photograph by Thomas Vivian.

Rear cover: Memorial to Edward I at Burgh-by-Sands.

First published 2008

Amberley Publishing Plc
Cirencester Road, Chalford,
Stroud, Gloucestershire, GL6 8PE

www.amberley-books.com

British Library Cataloguing in Publication Data.
A catalogue record for this book is available from the British Library.

ISBN 978 1 84868 230 6

Typesetting and Origination by Diagraf (www.diagraf.net)
Printed in Great Britain

Contents

Map 1: Sites in this book in Great Britain   4

Map 2: Sites in this book in France and Germany   5

Table of Kings and Queens   6

Introduction   10

The Kings and Queens   13

Sources of photographs   127

Further reading   128

Map 1: Sites in this book in Great Britain

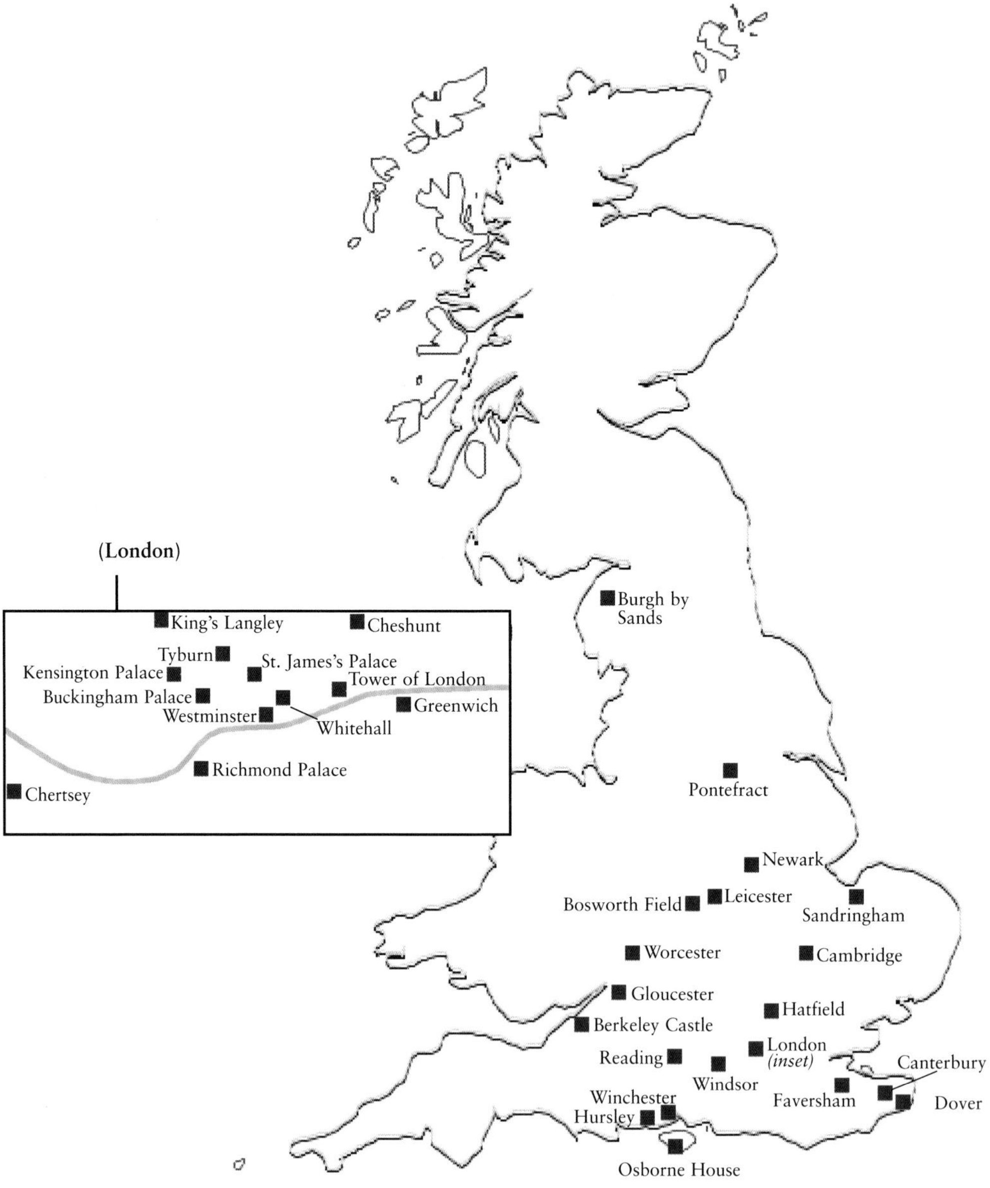

(London)

King's Langley Cheshunt

Tyburn
Kensington Palace St. James's Palace
Buckingham Palace Tower of London
Westminster Greenwich
Whitehall

Richmond Palace

Chertsey

Burgh by Sands

Pontefract

Newark

Bosworth Field Leicester
Sandringham

Worcester Cambridge

Gloucester
Berkeley Castle Hatfield

Reading London
(inset) Canterbury

Windsor
Winchester Faversham Dover
Hursley

Osborne House

Map 2: Sites in this book in France and Germany

Hanover

Osnabrück

St. Omer

Caen Rouen
Lyons la Forêt

St. Germain-en-Laye Paris

Vincennes

Chinon

Fontevrault

Châlus

Table of Kings and Queens

Name	Alternative or nicknames	Relation to predecessor	Born	Reigned from
William I	The Conqueror, The Bastard	Not close	Sep 1028	1066
William II	Rufus	3rd son	1056	1087
Henry I	Beauclerc, Lion of Justice	Brother	Sep 1068	1100
Stephen		Nephew	1097	1135
Henry II		1st cousin once removed	5 Mar 1133	1154
Richard I	Lionheart	3rd son	8 Sep 1157	1189
John	Lackland, Softsword	Brother	24 Dec 1166	1199
Henry III		1st son	10 Oct 1207	1216
Edward I	Hammer of the Scots, Longshanks	1st son	17 Jun 1239	1272
Edward II		4th son	25 Apr 1284	1307
Edward III		1st son	13 Nov 1312	1327
Richard II		Grandson	6 Jan 1367	1377
Henry IV		1st cousin	3 Apr 1367	1399
Henry V		1st son	9 Aug 1387	1413
Henry VI		Son	6 Dec 1421	1422
				1470
Edward IV		Distant cousin	28 Apr 1442	1461
				1471
Edward V	Prince in the Tower	1st son	2 Nov 1470	1483
Richard III		Uncle	2 Oct 1452	1483
Henry VII		Distant cousin	28 Jan 1457	1485
Henry VIII	Bluff King Hal	2nd son	28 Jun 1491	1509
Edward VI		Son	12 Oct 1537	1547

Reigned to	Years reigned	Died	Age at death	Died at	Principal resting place
1087	21	9 Sep 1087	59	St. Gervais, Rouen	Abbaye aux Hommes, Caen
1100	13	2 Aug 1100	44	New Forest	Winchester Cathedral
1135	35	1 Dec 1135	67	Lyons la Forêt	Reading Abbey
1154	19	25 Oct 1154	57	Dover Priory	Faversham
1189	35	6 Jul 1189	56	Chinon	Fontevrault Abbey
1199	10	6 Apr 1199	41	Chateau de Châlus	Fontevrault Abbey
1216	17	19 Oct 1216	49	Newark Castle	Worcester Cathedral
1272	56	16 Nov 1272	65	Palace of Westminster	Westminster Abbey
1307	35	7 Jul 1307	68	Burgh by Sands	Westminster Abbey
1327	20	21 Sep 1327	43	Berkeley Castle	Gloucester Cathedral
1377	50	22 Jun 1377	64	Richmond Palace	Westminster Abbey
1399	22	14 Feb 1400	33	Pontefract Castle	Westminster Abbey
1413	14	21 Mar 1413	45	Westminster Abbey	Canterbury Cathedral
1422	9	31 Aug 1422	35	Chateau de Vincennes	Westminster Abbey
1461					
1471	40	21 May 1471	49	Tower of London	St. George's Chapel, Windsor
1470					
1483	21	9 Apr 1483	40	Palace of Westminster	St. George's Chapel, Windsor
1483	2 months	? 1483	13	Tower of London?	Westminster Abbey?
1485	2	22 Aug 1485	32	Bosworth Field	Grey Friars Church, Leicester?
1509	24	21 Apr 1509	52	Richmond Palace	Westminster Abbey
1547	38	28 Jan 1547	55	Whitehall Palace	St. George's Chapel, Windsor
1553	6	6 Jul 1553	15	Greenwich Palace	Westminster Abbey

Name	Alternative or nicknames	Relation to predecessor	Born	Reigned from
Lady Jane Grey		1st cousin once removed	Oct 1537	1553
Mary I	Bloody Mary	1st cousin once removed	18 Feb 1516	1553
Elizabeth I	Virgin Queen, Gloriana	Half-sister	7 Sep 1533	1558
James I		Distant cousin	19 Jun 1566	1603
Charles I	The Martyr	2nd son	19 Nov 1600	1625
Oliver Cromwell	Lord Protector	None	25 Apr 1599	1653
Richard Cromwell	Tumbledown Dick, Queen Dick	3rd son	4 Oct 1626	1658
Charles II	The Merry Monarch, Old Rowley	2nd son (of Charles I)	29 May 1630	1660
James II		Brother	14 Oct 1633	1685
Mary II		1st daughter	30 Apr 1662	1689
William III		Nephew	14 Nov 1650	1689
Anne		Sister/sister-in-law	6 Feb 1665	1702
George I		1st cousin once removed	28 May 1660	1714
George II		Son	30 Oct 1683	1727
George III	Farmer George, Mad King George	Grandson	4 Jun 1738	1760
George IV	Prinny	1st son	12 Aug 1762	1820
William IV	Silly Billy	Brother	21 Aug 1765	1830
Victoria		Niece	24 May 1819	1837
Edward VII	Bertie	1st son	9 Nov 1841	1901
George V	The Sailor King	2nd son	3 Jun 1865	1910
Edward VIII		1st son	23 Jun 1894	1936
George VI		Brother	14 Dec 1895	1936

Reigned to	Years reigned	Died	Age at death	Died at	Principal resting place
1553	*c.*9 days	12 Feb 1554	16	Tower of London	Tower of London
1558	5	17 Nov 1558	42	St. James's Palace	Westminster Abbey
1603	45	24 Mar 1603	69	Richmond Palace	Westminster Abbey
1625	22	27 Mar 1625	58	Theobalds, Hatfield	Westminster Abbey
1649	24	30 Jan 1649	48	Whitehall Palace	St. George's Chapel, Windsor
1658	5	3 Sep 1658	59	Whitehall Palace	Tyburn
1659	1	12 Jul 1712	85	Cheshunt	Hursley Parish Church
1685	25	6 Feb 1685	54	Whitehall Palace	Westminster Abbey
1688	3	16 Sep 1701	67	St-Germain-en-Laye	St-Germain-en-Laye
1694	5	28 Dec 1694	32	Kensington Palace	Westminster Abbey
1702	13	8 Mar 1702	51	Kensington Palace	Westminster Abbey
1714	12	1 Aug 1714	49	Kensington Palace	Westminster Abbey
1727	13	11 Jun 1727	67	Osnabrück Castle	Herrenhäusen, Hanover
1760	33	25 Oct 1760	76	Kensington Palace	Westminster Abbey
1820	60	29 Jan 1820	81	Windsor Castle	St. George's Chapel, Windsor
1830	10	26 Jun 1830	67	Windsor Castle	St. George's Chapel, Windsor
1837	7	20 Jun 1837	71	Windsor Castle	St. George's Chapel, Windsor
1901	64	22 Jan 1901	81	Osborne House, IoW	Frogmore, Windsor
1910	9	6 May 1910	68	Buckingham Palace	St. George's Chapel, Windsor
1936	26	20 Jan 1936	70	Sandringham House	St. George's Chapel, Windsor
1936	11 months	28 May 1972	77	Bois de Boulogne	Frogmore, Windsor
1952	16	6 Feb 1952	56	Sandringham House	St. George's Chapel, Windsor

Introduction

'My name is Ozymandias, King of Kings:
Look on my works, ye Mighty, and despair!'
Nothing beside remains. Round the decay
Of that colossal wreck, boundless and bare,
The lone and level sands stretch far away.
(Percy Bysshe Shelley)

Kings and queens have always fascinated. They are central to every European country's history, and endowed with a mystique of power, glamour and fairytale. Naturally, historians pay most attention to their lives and achievements, but the death of a king or queen was a hugely important event at the time, often heralding revolution, invasion, dynastic change, radical new policies, unwonted alliances or civil war. Even when the transition was not so turbulent, passing safely from father to eldest son or other nominated heir, it was always a moment to mark, and a time to dust down the pomp and ceremony to show off at a funeral and coronation. Deaths rarely just 'happened' unless during an act of war. In the final months or years ministers, courtiers and heirs apparent would plan and plot, conspire and meddle, sometimes judiciously hastening the end, in order to safeguard their own position or protect the country from catastrophe. Foreign potentates took great interest in events, seeing an opportunity for a landgrab, or for an extension of their spheres of influence, or perhaps the need for heightened diplomatic niceties to prevent war with an aggressive successor. Magnates would take stock of their position, of how much favour they held with the successor, and whether their alliances and political scheming under their old master would spell danger for them under their new. The common people never greeted a monarch's demise with indifference; it was almost always a period of public mourning or rejoicing, whether real or enforced. It is easy to forget what impact a king or queen's death has, even in today's democratic society, when the last one in Britain occurred over fifty years ago.

Much can be learned about a king or queen from where they died. Edward I in Cumbria on his way to hammer the Scots. Richard the Lionheart in typical belligerent style pushing out his frontiers in the heart of the Limousin. Henry V pursuing his claim for the French throne, with unrelenting vigour, just outside Paris. George IV in his overly-ornate state apartments in Windsor Castle. George VI at his rural retreat in the rich hunting land of Norfolk. And what better place to contemplate the thoughts, actions and lives of these outstanding characters than at their tombs? Everlasting greatness was a desire common to many kings and queens. Sometimes this shines through in the splendid abbeys, chapels and tombs they helped design to house their mortal remains. Sometimes it's a perverse antithesis of all that they once were – an anonymous, half-worn slab of stone. You can ponder Henry I in the ruins of Reading Abbey, sad blocks of masonry that once formed the second largest abbey in England. Stephen lost forever in the pretty Kentish town of Faversham. John in isolated glory before the altar of Worcester Cathedral. Henry VII in his magnificent monument at the beating heart of British history, Westminster Abbey. Or Edward VIII seemingly still in partial exile in Frogmore. Following the trail of the deaths and burials of kings and queens leads you to some of the best corners of England (and France and Germany too!) This book will guide you to those places, whether you want to make a specific journey or just happen to be nearby. Almost all are fully accessible, most are proud of and knowledgeable about their royal association and do their best to welcome you to find out more.

Some monarchs are appealing, admirable characters. Others are repugnant. Likewise, some of the locations in this book are wonderful, evocative places, whilst others require a little more imagination to kindle the magic of history. All are worth a visit for anyone interested in royalty. To recommend a 'top five' I have to avoid any bias to a king or queen whom I find particularly colourful (and I admit to a penchant for Henrys I and II...) but I think these will provide much pleasure to almost anyone:

1. **Fontevrault Abbey.** A huge complex of monastic buildings from across the centuries, all built in a serene yet stark white stone. The painted effigies of Henry II and his rebellious son Richard I lie in peaceful harmony in the nave of the otherwise empty church. Could such still figures really represent the fizzing, brutal and ambitious characters we know they once were?

2. **Westminster Abbey.** Stunning architecture, overflowing with statues, tombs and memorials to the famous and worthy of the country. No trip to visit royalty is complete without a specially guided tour to the heart of the abbey, the shrine of Edward the Confessor. Here you can gaze (or rather attempt to gaze, as it is rather high up) at possibly the most moving tomb effigy of them all – Henry III.

3. **Edward I monument.** So near yet so far. The aged Edward was on his way to quell the Scots forever, but died within sight of Scotland, at the furthest outreach of his kingdom. With him died the hopes of northern Englishmen, and consigned the region to centuries of border raids and pillaging. The monument is in the midst of the salt marshes of the Solway Firth, with little around it but birdsong and the tugging wind.

4. **The Rufus Stone.** Not far from a busy trunk road in the New Forest, a most unlikely setting for a royal death. But is there an unsolved mystery of royal murder and treachery here, or was it really just an accident? We'll never know of course, but it's certainly one of the best signposted and most well-visited sites, for perhaps the least-known of all our monarchs. And there are few better spots for a walk and a picnic than the New Forest.

5. **Tyburn.** Not because it's beautiful, or particularly interesting. In fact there are few sites in this book that are less appealing. Rather because you hear so much about the infamous hanging tree of Tyburn, but its location is rarely given. If you successfully navigate the busy roads (there are no crossing points) and ignore the litter and weeds on the traffic island, you'll find a nice little circular stone marking the spot, and you have to imagine quite hard that Oliver Cromwell's body lies somewhere near...

Wherever you go, I hope your regal travels give as much enjoyment as they did to me.

Notes

i) This book is concerned only with kings and queens regnant from William the Conqueror onwards, although there is a rich history of kings prior to the Norman invasion. I have used the term 'English' fairly loosely here, primarily to distinguish from the Scottish monarchy. The kingdom evolved significantly to include and lose all or part of France, Wales, Scotland and Ireland. England is the main constant through all 886 years of the book, and the terms British or United Kingdom only apply later on.

ii) Although our two Lord Protectors were not 'royal' they occupied the position of monarch in pretty much all but name. Oliver Cromwell even took to wearing purple and sitting in state to receive visitors. I have therefore included them. Besides, they make for very interesting subjects.

iii) Whereas monarchs died in just the one place, they are often buried in several places! Almost all kings and queens up to a certain period were embalmed, sometimes to allow the body to lie in state, sometimes to allow the body to be carried to its tomb, a journey which could take several days or weeks. Early kings also had a godlike status, so embalming was a way to achieving a more lasting presence on earth. The innards were cut out and often buried nearby, or placed in an urn and taken somewhere of personal or political significance. This book guides you to the burial sites of hearts, brains and other organs where known, and where it adds something of interest to the journey. This can, for example with James II and Oliver Cromwell, lead to multiple sites.

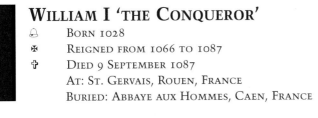

The Kings and Queens

WILLIAM I 'THE CONQUEROR'

⌂ BORN 1028

✠ REIGNED FROM 1066 TO 1087

✝ DIED 9 SEPTEMBER 1087

AT: ST. GERVAIS, ROUEN, FRANCE

BURIED: ABBAYE AUX HOMMES, CAEN, FRANCE

All English monarchs right through to Elizabeth II can trace their lineage back to William the Conqueror. He was a highly ambitious and often cruel man, who rose to become King of England despite being the illegitimate son of a Norman duke whose antecedents were Viking raiders and vassals of the King of France. William's epithet 'the Conqueror' goes far beyond the impressive feat of invading England and defeating King Harold's army at Hastings. He utterly changed England – introducing a feudal system, creating new laws, building castles, replacing Anglo-Saxon nobility with Norman-French and laying the foundations for the language we now call English.

William's upbringing moulded his character. Inheriting his father's dukedom as a fifteen year old bastard (much of the aristocracy refused to recognise his rights) he faced constant rebellion and the threat of invasion. Three of his guardians were killed protecting him before he finally asserted authority. His early life was about learning to survive in a brutal and hostile environment, in which he was successful due to his physical strength, savagery and leadership abilities. He brought all these to bear at his most famous victory in 1066, where he led much of the fighting personally, displaying himself on horseback to his soldiers to disprove rumours that he had been killed. The twenty-one years of his reign were spent mostly in crushing Anglo-Saxon resistance. He laid waste swathes of Yorkshire, pursued rebels in East Anglia and in 1085 commissioned a survey of the whole country to maximise tax revenues – known later as the Domesday Book.

Whilst William is most famous as the first numbered King of England, the last and most successful conqueror of our land, he considered himself first and foremost as Duke of Normandy. It was during an attempt to expand his continental territory that, in 1087, reducing Mantes to ruins, his horse trod on hot ashes and threw him. Suffering severe abdominal injuries, William was taken to the priory of St. Gervais on the outskirts of his Norman capital Rouen where he died ten days later on 9 September. The priory is no longer, but there is still an austere Norman church on the site, on Rue Claude Groulard, with a plaque commemorating William's death. Also, above the south entrance, there is another plaque claiming that William's last words were "Justice, right and peace with God".

William's body suffered from turmoil in death as in life. Having been abandoned by his sons (rushing off to claim their inheritances) and his nobles (rushing off to protect their lands from feared anarchy) the dead William was stripped of all his clothes and possessions. A local

ICI ÉTAIT
LE PRIEURÉ DE SAINT GERVAIS
OÙ MOURUT
GUILLAUME LE CONQUÉRANT
LE IX SEPTEMBRE
MLXXXVII

ACADEMIA ROTH· POSUIT AN· MDCCCXLVI

1. Plaque on the west side of the Church of St. Gervais, Rouen. 'Here was the Priory of Saint Gervais where William the Conqueror died on 9 September 1087'.

2. The magnificent Abbaye aux Hommes with its church of St. Stephen, built in the same mellow, light-coloured stone as the rest of the city of Caen.

man arranged for the body to be taken for burial to Caen, to the church of St. Stephen in the Abbaye aux Hommes, the monastery which William had established in return for being dis-excommunicated by the pope.

There, his burial service was interrupted by a local knight claiming compensation for lands taken unjustly from him by William, and by the bloated body bursting as they tried to force it into the small stone coffin, causing a severe stench that hurried the rituals along irreligiously. Various people have since interfered with his body and with the original monument raised in his memory by his son William Rufus. Calvinists scattered his bones in the sixteenth century, with the exception of a single thighbone. This bone was re-buried, lying under various monuments, one of which was destroyed by revolutionaries in 1783. In 1987 the French authorities declared the thighbone to be a true relic of William the Conqueror and laid a simple stone slab over his supposed burial site.

The abbey is easy to find, at the west end of the main shopping street of St. Pierre. The walk from the Abbaye aux Dames, founded by William's queen and at the east end of the street, is well worth it, passing the castle, numerous old alleys and bustling coffee shops. The church is more accessible than the abbey itself, and once inside, head for the altar where the marble tombstone is well signposted.

3. William's monument in front of the altar. The inscription reads: 'The indomitable William the Conqueror, Duke of the Normans, King of the English, is buried here. Founder of this House, he died here, 1087'. Note the inaccuracy – he died in Rouen!

WILLIAM II 'RUFUS'

⌂   BORN 1056
✠   REIGNED FROM 1087 TO 1100
✟   DIED 2 AUGUST 1100
     IN: THE NEW FOREST
     BURIED: WINCHESTER CATHEDRAL

A king whose most memorable event was his death! Called Rufus after the reddish colour of his complexion (his hair was blonde) William II inherited England's throne upon the death of his father William the Conqueror. His older brother Robert was given Normandy, his younger brother Henry was given a considerable sum of money, and consequently there was much fighting between the hot-headed siblings. War, rebellion and repression characterised much of William's short and unpopular reign.

William was a stocky, ferocious warrior with a quick temper to match. Much loved and respected by his soldiers, he did little to overcome his many weaknesses as a king. As a homosexual, or possibly a bisexual, William was reviled by his god-fearing medieval subjects. He hated the church, antagonising his bishops and even the pope by abusing church revenues. He imposed heavy taxes in England to fuel his power struggles, yet scorned the recently conquered Anglo-Saxon nobility who paid them.

There is much mystery surrounding his death. What we do know is that he died whilst hunting somewhere in the New Forest from an arrow, or crossbow bolt, in his chest. The official story at the time was that he was accidentally killed by Sir Walter Tyrrell, his sole companion, who shot at and missed a stag but hit his king, either directly or by deflection off a tree. This version was supported by his brother Henry, unsurprisingly given the latter's desire for a succession untroubled by rumours of intrigue and murder. Yet many questions lie unanswered. Why was the king alone with just one companion? Where was the rest of the hunting party? Not one of this party stopped to tend the dead king's body, including Henry who went directly to Winchester to seize the treasury and have himself appointed king with indecent, and perhaps planned, haste.

Tyrrell himself fled abroad, and was unpursued. In fear of his life for his mistake, or paid to stay away by Henry? William's older brother Robert, and his appointed successor, was on crusade and in no position to challenge Henry for the throne. Most modern speculation points to Henry as the probable instigator of his death, but we are unlikely ever to know. William's body was left in the New Forest for local people to drag in a cart to Winchester, where he was buried in St. Swithun's church, part of the new Norman cathedral being built on the site of the old Anglo-Saxon minster. Few mourned his death, and even fewer at his funeral.

For a king who is little known today, the place of his death and burial are surprisingly easy to find. The Rufus Stone is a triangular monument erected in the eighteenth century, later encased in iron, to mark the site of the tree that supposedly deflected the deadly arrow. It is signposted from the A31 and is opposite an eponymous car park. Like the manner of his death there is much speculation about the exact location. Almost certainly this is not it, but it is a good tribute, and the words on the monument bear a few moments' reading. Nearby is the Sir Walter Tyrrell pub with a fine sign showing the dying king.

For many years a large stone coffin in the centre of the quire of Winchester Cathedral was thought to contain William's remains, but is now considered to hold those of Henry of Blois, a bishop. In the last century the bones were dug up, found to contain an arrow head, and re-buried without any firm conclusion either way.

There are also six mortuary chests on top of the screen around the quire. At some point William's remains may have been moved into these. In the seventeenth century Parliamentarian soldiers opened the chests and scattered the bones, throwing some to smash the cathedral's stained glass windows. The bones were put back haphazardly into the chests, and it is thought that William's may lie here mixed with the relics of King Egbert and other Anglo-Saxon royals. If true, this is one of the few places where you have to look up to see an English king's final resting place.

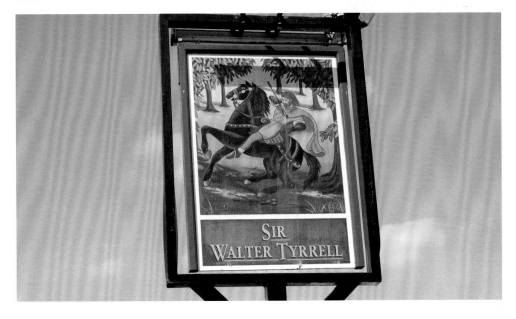

HERE STOOD
THE OAK TREE,
ON WHICH AN ARROW
SHOT BY
SIR WALTER TYRRELL
AT A STAG,
GLANCED AND STRUCK
KING WILLIAM
THE SECOND,
SURNAMED RUFUS,
ON THE BREAST,
OF WHICH HE
INSTANTLY DIED,
ON THE SECOND
DAY OF AUGUST,
ANNO 1100.

Right: 4. The Rufus Stone in the New Forest.

Below: 5. The Sir Walter Tyrrell pub sign, near the Rufus Stone; surely the only pub sign celebrating a monarch's death?

SIR
WALTER TYRRELL

6. The quire and nave of Winchester Cathedral showing William II's former tomb in the centre.

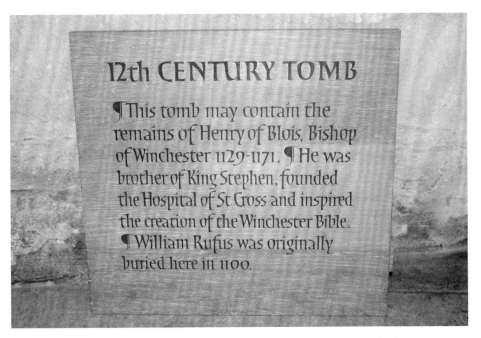

12th CENTURY TOMB

¶ This tomb may contain the remains of Henry of Blois, Bishop of Winchester 1129-1171. ¶ He was brother of King Stephen, founded the Hospital of St Cross and inspired the creation of the Winchester Bible. ¶ William Rufus was originally buried here in 1100.

7. The panel by the tomb showing William II, King of England, as a footnote to the former Bishop of Winchester, Henry of Blois.

8. William's chest is the nearest to the tomb on the south side of the screen.

HENRY I 'BEAUCLERC'

⌂   BORN 1068
✠   REIGNED FROM 1100 TO 1135
✝   DIED 1 DECEMBER 1135
      AT: LYONS LA FORÊT, EURE, FRANCE
      BURIED: READING ABBEY

Henry, fourth son of the Conqueror and one of the most effective early kings of England, was nicknamed 'Beauclerc' for his scholarly achievements, in Latin, Norman-French and, importantly, English. It was said that he was at home with a falcon on one hand and a book in the other. He did much to improve relations between his Norman and Anglo-Saxon subjects. Not only was he born in England, he married Edith, a descendant of the royal Anglo-Saxon line, and re-took Normandy from his brother Robert, achieving a kind of reversal of the events of 1066. He established a good system of administration for his expanded territories, creating a bureaucracy that would dispense justice, collect taxes and manage the treasury on his behalf. He also introduced a forerunner of the Magna Carta - the Charter of Liberties – to address certain abuses of royal power against both state and church. His other nickname 'Lion of Justice' underlines his reputation as a progressive, reforming king.

Although his marriage to Edith was a happy and successful one, Henry was a serial adulterer. He sired over 20 illegitimate children, the most by an English monarch. Despite this prodigious paternal effort, and due to the tragic drowning of his only surviving legitimate son in 1120, his main legacy to the country was an uncertain succession which led to nearly twenty years of civil war.

9. Lyons la Forêt, one of the most beautiful villages in Normandy.

Right: 10. Henry I is well-remembered in Lyons la Forêt. Little remains of his castle, but some of the walls can be seen behind this memorial at the foot of the Rue de l'Hôtel de Ville. There is also a hotel called 'Les Lions de Beauclerc'.

Below: 11. Reading Abbey: picturesque ruins of a place that was once one of the wealthiest abbeys in England.

12. A strange choice of Celtic cross for a Norman King of an Anglo-Saxon country. It was raised in 1909 in the pleasure gardens that stand on part of the site of the former abbey.

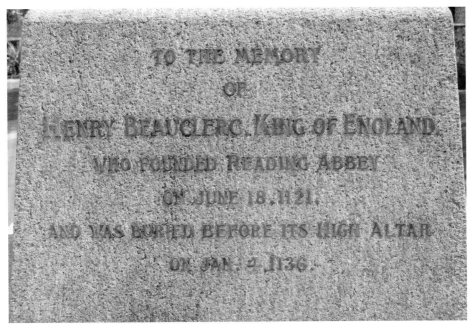

13. The inscription on Henry's cross displaying the moniker 'Beauclerc', of which he was very proud.

14. The plaque indicating that Henry was buried nearby.

On 1 August 1135 Henry travelled to Normandy to visit his daughter and recognised heir, Matilda, his son-in-law Geoffrey of Anjou and their two children. An eclipse the following day was seen as a bad omen. Henry argued excessively with his daughter but was very fond of his grandchildren, dandling the future King Henry II on his knee. He also fought with Geoffrey, who had started intriguing against him, with an eye on ruling England through Matilda. After a day spent hunting in the beech forest near his castle in Lyons la Forêt he indulged in his favourite dish of lampreys, possibly as a guest of the Cistercian monks of the Abbaye de Mortemer, which he had founded in 1130. His physicians had expressly forbidden him from eating this dish (or so they claimed afterwards to avoid blame or accusations of poisoning) but being a stubborn sixty-six year old king with the typical determined temperament of the Norman line, he ignored their advice.

Lampreys are a type of parasitic eel, sucking blood from their fish hosts, and were much favoured as a delicacy in medieval times. Unfortunately they are very fatty and difficult to digest. Henry, otherwise a still powerful and much respected king, became unwell, fell into a fever and within six days died famously of 'a surfeit of lampreys' in his castle. Similarities perhaps to the later King John, who was rumoured to have died from a 'surfeit of peaches', and who also left his kingdom subject to anarchy and civil war.

Many cathedrals and abbeys clamoured to have King Henry I's remains interred within their walls, but the king had had time to finalise his burial plans, and in the end his body was taken to Rouen Cathedral where it was crudely mummified, wrapped in ox hides, and transported back to Reading Abbey in England.

The remains of his body were laid to rest under the high altar of the church of the nascent Cluniac abbey which he had founded in 1121. His funeral was attended by the new King Stephen and Henry's widow Queen Adeliza, who gave a hundred shillings for a lamp to burn constantly over his grave.

The abbey church was not consecrated until 1164, but happily in the presence of his grandson Henry II and Thomas à Becket. Reading Abbey grew to be a wealthy and influential institution but after Henry VIII's reformation was piece by piece ripped down to build, amongst others, the churches of St. Mary and St. Laurence, and was finally ravaged during the 1643 Parliamentary siege of the town.

Henry's tomb was broken open at some time in the sixteenth century by people searching for a legendary silver coffin as well as for further building material. His bones are thought to have been scattered, and there is sadly little proof today of the presence of one of England's great early kings. There is a large Celtic cross in his memory on the site of the former north-west front (now Forbury Gardens), and a small plaque in the ruins of the south transept, near St. James RC Church.

STEPHEN

⚮ BORN 1097
✲ REIGNED FROM 1135 TO 1154
✝ DIED 25 OCTOBER 1154
AT: DOVER PRIORY
BURIED: FAVERSHAM ABBEY

'In the days of this King there was nothing but strife, evil, and robbery, for quickly the great men who were traitors rose against him. When the traitors saw that Stephen was a good-humoured, kindly, and easy-going man who inflicted no punishment, then they committed all manner of horrible crimes . . . And so it lasted for nineteen years while Stephen was King, till the land was all undone and darkened with such deeds, and men said openly that Christ and his angels slept.' So says the Anglo-Saxon Chronicle of a king with a perhaps unjustly bad personal reputation, whose anarchic reign fell between two of the strongest monarchs England has known.

Stephen was generally considered to be a pleasant, convivial man and not unskilled with a sword. A grandson of William the Conqueror, he was a protégé of Henry I; he was one of the richest and most influential men in England, and may have thought that he was being raised to succeed his uncle. However Henry knew that Stephen did not have the character to be king. He was too affable and neither decisive nor forceful. Despite having sworn fealty three times to Henry's daughter and nominated heir, Stephen rushed to secure the throne for himself upon Henry's death. The consequences were terrible for England, with local barons building hundreds of castles, ravaging the local peasantry and enforcing their own rules. The ensuing struggle with his rival for the throne, Henry's daughter Matilda, led to years of siege and counter-siege, and cloaked flight from one another through the snowy landscape of Oxfordshire.

Of Stephen's last days little is recorded. In 1153 he agreed the Treaty of Wallingford with his cousin, the future Henry II. Stephen was to remain king for the rest of his days but recognised Henry as his rightful heir, thus ending the civil war. From then on he appeared to be growing in stature as sovereign, enjoying popular support as well as that of his noblemen, and issuing new coinage from mints around the country. Yet, in 1152 his beloved wife Matilda had died, and in 1153 his eldest son Eustace. Some reports say he was a broken man, but in deeds he appeared to be stronger than ever.

Stephen died suddenly of an apoplexy or heart attack on 25 October 1154 at Dover Priory. Although the Priory has been largely demolished there are still three original buildings in an excellent, well-renovated state, used by Dover College for various purposes. It is uncertain exactly where Stephen died but it is possible that he was in the Guest House, which is now used as a chapel by the school and behind which lies 'King Stephen's Garden'.

Stephen was buried alongside his wife at Faversham Abbey in Kent, just a few miles from Dover on the route to London through Canterbury. He had founded the abbey in 1147 in dedication to the house of Blois (his father was Count of Blois) in the hope that his dynasty would rule over England for centuries. The abbey was dissolved in 1538 as part of Henry VIII's reformation and the buildings largely dismantled by 1671, although a few fifteenth-century farm buildings survive today. During excavations in 1964 two empty pits were found at the centre of the former abbey church quire. Much of the land has been built on, or is in private hands, but there are plenty of reminders of the abbey in Faversham itself.

There are two legends about what happened to Stephen's remains when the abbey church was dismantled. One says that the bones were re-buried in the parish church of St. Mary of Charity,

15. The original twelfth-century Guest House of Dover Priory, now used as a chapel by Dover College.

FAVERSHAM ABBEY INNER GATEWAY
FOUNDED 1147, DEMOLISHED 1771

THE SALVAGED MASONRY WAS
RE-USED IN THE CONSTRUCTION
OF 63-64 ABBEY STREET.
BETWEEN THIS POINT AND THE
PRESENT 'ANCHOR' TAVERN WAS
THE ABBEY'S NETHER GREEN.

16. One of several plaques marking former abbey buildings in the very picturesque town of Faversham.

Right: 17. The canopy tomb and Stephen brass in St. Mary, Faversham. There is a carved face of a king amongst other images around the edge of the canopy.

Below: 18. Faversham Creek. The lasting resting place of King Stephen?

in the Trinity Chapel to the east of the chancel. It is a fascinating church, full of medieval marvels. There is a brass on an unmarked canopy tomb to mark his possible last resting place.

The second legend relates that Stephen's bones were simply thrown into Faversham Creek. Once the lifeblood of the town, the creek still has some commercial value but is used today mostly for pleasure boats and for scenic walks, and on a calm day seems a perfectly peaceful place for a king's 'tomb'.

19. The massive castle at Chinon on the Vienne, near to its junction with the Loire.

HENRY II

⚭ BORN 1133
✠ REIGNED FROM 1154 TO 1189
✝ DIED 6 JULY 1189
    AT: CHINON, INDRE-ET-LOIRE, FRANCE
    BURIED: FONTEVRAULT ABBEY, MAINE-ET-LOIRE, FRANCE

Henry was as effective as his predecessor Stephen had been ineffectual. He was descended from William the Conqueror and the Norman line through his mother, but took his dynastic Plantagenet name from his father, the Count of Anjou – the name comes from the Latin for broom 'planta genista', the family emblem carried to war on Angevin battle helmets. A man of quite astounding energy, Henry devoted himself to restoring law and order in England following the anarchy of his predecessor's reign and to establishing control over what was, at the time, the largest empire in Europe. Although comfortable with, and indeed keen to indulge in, the company of nearly everyone – scholars, soldiers, philosophers, taverners – Henry confided in few. Those he did confide in had a profound impact on his rule: his wife, the equally astute and domineering Eleanor of Aquitaine, his lover Rosamund de Clifford, and his mentor/friend/administrator, later enemy, Thomas à Becket.

Henry's closest relationships had a habit of turning sour. The most famous of these of course ended in the murder, unwitting or not, of Becket in Canterbury Cathedral. Henry's reputation in Europe never fully recovered from the stain of Becket's martyrdom, and his rebellious sons remorselessly exploited this chink in his armour. His sons never ceased to be a thorn in his side, encouraged as they were by their mother Eleanor. She and Henry had a tempestuous relationship, flamed by their matching quick tempers and iron wills, and by his serial adultery. Ten years in prison, by order of her husband, did little to quell her ambitions.

20. The flagstone in Chinon castle marking the exact site of Henry's death.

21. Tomb effigy of Henry II (and Eleanor of Aquitaine) in Fontevrault Abbey.

As he grew older, debilitating bouts of depression increasingly took their toll. He had had a remarkable constitution, but this was eventually worn down by his attempts to be everywhere all the time and by a familial tendency to fatness in old age. In the summer of 1189 Henry had to go to the defence of Anjou, where he suffered defeat at Le Mans at the hands of his sons Richard and John, abetted by Philip Augustus, King of France. Shamed, bruised and physically weak, Henry was defiant to the last, reportedly giving Richard a kiss of peace whilst breathing into his ear "God grant that I die not until I have avenged myself on thee". He retreated to his castle at Chinon where he died of a fever, probably brought on by his manic depression and the strain of keeping his territories together.

The castle now is a well preserved ruin, though subject to questionable renovation and redevelopment. It is easy to see how important it was in Henry's day, a bastion of power on the southern edge of his empire. The site is impressive, dominating the river and the grey slated roofs of the medieval village below, and definitely worth exploring. Inside the Middle Castle is a flagstone marking the exact site where Henry died, in the chapel of St. Mélaine, whose walls are no longer visible.

Having been laid out in the chapel and stripped bare by his servants, his body was taken to nearby Fontevrault Abbey by his loyal yet illegitimate son Geoffrey. The abbey today is one of the largest and best preserved in France, with a colourful history. It was built over 900 years ago partly as a mausoleum for the Angevins, and was a seat of Plantagenet power and learning for centuries. The abbey church where you can find Henry's tomb effigy is a remarkably bright, empty place, a strange mixture of Norman and Byzantine-inspired architecture. Henry's splendid coloured effigy lies next to his estranged wife Eleanor's, in a sealed-off area in the nave that also contains figures of Richard the Lionheart and Isabella of Angoulême. The effect of these coloured figures amidst the near-white stonework is striking. The exact location of the tombs is unknown, and the effigies themselves have been moved several times.

Despite his many administrative achievements (for which today's England has many reasons to be thankful) Henry died a sad man, cursing himself for his failures, a sorrowful contrast to the energetic twenty-one year old who had blasted his way into the English monarchy some thirty-five years previously.

RICHARD I 'THE LIONHEART'

🔔 BORN 1157

✠ REIGNED FROM 1189 TO 1199

✟ DIED 6 APRIL 1199

AT: CHÂLUS, HAUTE-VIENNE, FRANCE

BURIED: FONTEVRAULT ABBEY, MAINE-ET-LOIRE, FRANCE. HEART IN ROUEN CATHEDRAL, SEINE-MARITIME, FRANCE; ENTRAILS IN CHÂLUS; BRAIN IN CHARROUX ABBEY, VIENNE, FRANCE.

Richard, six feet five inches tall, third son of Henry II and Eleanor of Aquitaine, was a warrior king and Plantagenet par excellence. He earned his sobriquet 'Lionheart' from his dedication to chivalric ideals and military prowess, but was also fiery-tempered, cruel and prone to poor political judgment. Of his nine and a half years rule, he spent just a year on English soil, using his kingdom's revenues to finance his crusade in the Near East and latterly the expansion of his Norman and Angevin territories at the expense of King Philip of France. He very nearly bankrupted England to pay his ransom after being captured by the Austrian Duke Leopold on his way back from the crusade. Beloved by his mother and in open rebellion against his father, 'Good King Richard's' renown has been enhanced hugely by his heroic nickname, the endless romanticism of nineteenth-century writers, and by comparison to his considerably less chivalric brother and successor 'Bad King John'. Less well known is that Richard was almost certainly a homosexual, who shared a bed with Philip of France, leaving his wife Berengaria (whom he married while still formally engaged to another) distraught and childless.

Richard was made for war, and pursued it with great zeal all his life, fighting against his father, his former lover, his brother and of course the Saracens. Even when he succumbed to the traditional Norman/Plantagenet fatness in later life he still led from the front, careless for his own safety. It was whilst besieging the castle of Châlus in the Limousin, now in the Département of Haute-Vienne, in France, that he was wounded by a bolt or arrow from the walls. An incompetent surgeon mangled his flesh while pulling out the bolt head, which turned the wound gangrenous. Richard succumbed quickly, summoning his mother, Eleanor of Aquitaine, to what he knew would be his death-bed. Legend has it that he pardoned the archer who had shot the fatal bolt while the rest of the castle inhabitants were slaughtered upon its capture. Richard died on 6 April in his mother's arms. The archer died soon afterwards, flayed alive by Richard's vengeful troops.

The ruins of the castle, and the chapel where Richard's entrails are buried, are unfortunately in private hands and not open to visitors. However there is a small museum nearby, many references to Richard in the streets and restaurants, and a picturesque Route du Richard Coeur-de-Lion linking Châlus with numerous castles in the lush Limousin countryside.

Eleanor accompanied her son's body to the ancestral Fontevrault Abbey where he was buried inside the church in a penitent position, near his father Henry. The site of the tomb itself is unknown as the remains disappeared during the French revolution, but Richard's stone effigy is in a relatively good condition, lying next to the smaller wooden one of Isabella of Angoulême, wife of his younger brother King John.

Two parts of his innards were sent elsewhere. His brain is buried in the abbey at Charroux in the Poitou, an insult to the people's treachery towards him. Richard's heart however lies in Rouen Cathedral, ancestral capital of his Norman forefathers. The tomb is easy to find, on the south side of the choir, just past the tomb of Rollo, first Duke of Normandy. At Richard's feet is a lion, and the inscription on the side reads: 'Here lies the heart of Richard, King of the English, who was called lion heart. He died in the year 1199.'

22. Châlus-Chabrol castle. The keep, remains of some walls and a few more recent buildings look down on the ruined castle of Châlus-Maulmont in the foreground.

23. The nave of the church at Fontevrault Abbey, housing four Plantagenet tomb effigies.

24. The coloured tomb effigy of Richard 'Coeur de Lion' (behind Isabella's) at Fontevrault Abbey.

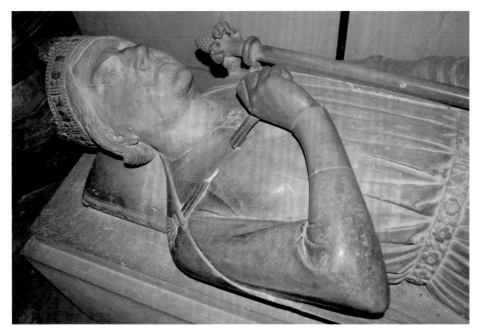

25. The splendid effigy lying over Richard's heart in Rouen. The tomb is well sign-posted within the cathedral.

JOHN 'LACKLAND' AND 'SOFTSWORD'

    🔔   BORN 1166

    ✠   REIGNED FROM 1199 TO 1216

    ✝   DIED 19 OCTOBER 1216

         AT: NEWARK CASTLE

         BURIED: WORCESTER CATHEDRAL

Like Stephen before him, John is another English king with a disastrous reputation. For a number of reasons however, John is the more well-known. He was the treacherous younger brother of the much (and unjustly) loved Richard the Lionheart; he was forced to sign the Magna Carta, one of the greatest documents in social and legal history; and of course he plays a key role in the fable of Robin Hood... Some historians have recently tried to salvage John's name, and with some justification. He was his father's favourite, a man of considerable literary taste, at times a reasonable governor, and certainly intelligent. But John was also sly, quick-tempered, often lavish and conceited. His nicknames of 'Softsword' and 'Lackland' point to his military and political failings, and he must surely be judged on the paltry achievements of his reign.

John was never popular due both to his personality and to the fact that he should not have been king in the first place. Arthur, son of John's older, deceased brother Geoffrey was regarded by many as the legitimate heir to Richard I. Sponsored by the ever-opportunistic French King Philip Augustus, Arthur waged war against John for five years. By the end of the war not only had England lost the French and Norman domains consolidated by Henry II, but John had killed his young nephew, reportedly with his own hands. Nobles and peasants alike were horrified, but John surpassed it by falling out with the Pope over the appointment of Stephen Langton as Archbishop of Canterbury. He received a papal interdict for his temerity, so that for many years weddings, Christian burials and other important religious sacraments could not be performed

26. Newark Castle overlooking the River Trent. It was built by Bishop Alexander 'the Magnificent' in the twelfth century and destroyed after the Civil War in the seventeenth.

27. John's tomb effigy in Worcester Cathedral.

28. The lion eating John's sword.

in England. The population was incensed. Landowners and nobility also riled against ever-increasing taxes. John responded with murder, threats and a network of spies, undermining yet further his reputation.

Eventually, in 1215, the barons forced John to sign a great charter, the Magna Carta, recognising the power of the law over the king's arbitrary whims. Although primarily intended to restore baronial rights, it demonstrated germinal feelings of collective responsibility for the nation's welfare, and is an important foundation of modern law and democracy. John's death in 1216 followed his inevitable rebuttal of the Magna Carta and the resulting rebellion. Fighting simultaneously the French Dauphin (installed by some barons as king in London), the Scottish King Alexander (welcomed as lord over northern England by local landowners), and well-armed, disloyal nobles in other parts of the country, John wandered from safe-house to safe-house with his baggage train. Famously losing his crown and other regalia in the Wash, and under severe strain, John fell to overeating. An excess of peaches and new cider at Swinshed is blamed for the severe stomach pains that beset him, but it could have been disease or poison – chroniclers of his age were keen to label an unpopular king as having caused his own death by gluttony.

John was moved to Newark Castle, which was kept by men still loyal to him. Here he died four days later, in agony and during a severe storm. The castle makes for good viewing, set as it is by the river and in the middle of the pleasant market town of Newark with its fascinating Civil War history. John is alleged to have died in the south west tower (at the far right of the photo) but he is more likely to have died in the gatehouse (towards the left of the photo) where rooms for important guests were kept. Although the castle was largely destroyed in the seventeenth century by Parliamentarian forces, and then by builders seeking stone, both the gatehouse and remaining towers can be visited on request.

One of his last wishes was to be buried at the shrine of St. Wulfstan in Worcester Cathedral. Wulfstan was a renowned bishop of Worcester, canonised during John's reign, and therefore of deep personal significance to him.

The tomb is well-signposted, lying in the quire in front of the altar, not far from the last resting place of Prince Arthur, Henry VIII's older brother. The effigy shows John with the two smaller figures of Saints Oswald and Wulfstan at his shoulders, and is the original, though the sarcophagus, with gold English leopards on red shields, was rebuilt in the sixteenth century. The lid is made of Purbeck marble, lending a decorative, almost mosaic-like appearance, and is in a remarkably good state. It was painted in medieval times but you could argue that the polished stone is more moving in its simplicity. A lion at John's feet is eating his sword – a somewhat paradoxical symbolism of bravery for a king whose nickname was 'Softsword'.

His heart is said to have been buried in the Angevin abbey at Fontevrault, but there is no evidence of this today.

HENRY III

⚱ BORN 1207
✠ REIGNED FROM 1216 TO 1272
✝ DIED 16 NOVEMBER 1272
AT: PALACE OF WESTMINSTER
BURIED: WESTMINSTER ABBEY

Having come to the throne at the age of nine, Henry III went on to become one of England's longest reigning monarchs. At first glance this would indicate stability and perhaps a renaissance in the status of the crown, so thoroughly debased by Henry's reviled father John. Little could be further from the truth. Henry was simple, unable to govern his country or even his own finances. His reign was dominated by unsuccessful wars, baronial intrigue and a deep dissatisfaction amongst the general population with the achievements of their pathetic ruler.

Yet, in an odd way, Henry's legacy is more obvious today than that of many more powerful English kings from those early centuries. Henry's passions were religion and art. He completely rebuilt Westminster Abbey, which had been established by his patron saint, King Edward the Confessor. He built, or rebuilt, the Great Hall in Winchester, and the cathedrals in Wells, Salisbury and Lincoln. Religious orders, centres of learning and artists began to flourish with his encouragement. He had a loving relationship with a strong wife (Eleanor of Provence) who bore him nine children, the eldest of whom became the great Edward I, a godsend to a weakened England.

Moreover, the council of magnates who had begun to govern the country during Richard I's lengthy absences, and developed their rights under John through the Magna Carta, found that they could hone their powers yet more under such a weak-minded king as Henry. This was an important phase in the transferral of power from a single, omnipotent, hereditary ruler towards a more democratic (though not at all elected) style of government. In Henry III's reign the Magna Carta was re-confirmed, and the Provisions of Oxford gave further control over taxation and governance to a parliamentary council.

Henry had been pursuing his religious devotions when taken ill at Bury St. Edmunds. He hurried back to London, fearing his time was come and wishing to be closer to the shrine he had built for his beloved Edward the Confessor. He died, aged 65, in his palace at Westminster. His body was buried close to the Confessor's shrine in the very heart of Westminster Abbey.

Henry was the first numbered monarch to be buried at Westminster Abbey, establishing it as a mausoleum for the English monarchy. His effigy is very moving, in its gilt simplicity. The man looks meek and kindly, rather than majestic. A true realisation perhaps? Henry's heart is supposed to have been buried in the Angevin abbey at Fontevrault, but as with his father John's, there is little evidence today.

Little missed by his people, Henry was much mourned by his son Edward I who had effectively ruled for the last eight years of Henry's reign, and who patently admired his father for what he was, rather than condemning him for what he lacked.

Right: 29. Henry
III's tomb close to
the rebuilt shrine of
Edward the Confessor
in Westminster Abbey.

Below: 30. Fontevrault
Abbey, possibly home
to Henry III's heart,
but certainly home
to earlier Plantagenet
kings.

EDWARD I 'LONGSHANKS' AND 'HAMMER OF THE SCOTS'

- ⚲ BORN 1239
- ✠ REIGNED FROM 1272 TO 1307
- ☦ DIED 7 JULY 1307
  AT: BURGH-BY-SANDS, CUMBRIA
  BURIED: WESTMINSTER ABBEY

Edward I is a very appealing character from a historical perspective, and one of England's greatest monarchs. After John and Henry III England was in sore need of a powerful king. Governance was slack, there was much in-fighting between the barons, and the people were losing their faith in the monarchy. Edward was physically powerful and combative, reminiscent of Richard the Lionheart, but combined this with a passion for improving and expanding his kingdom. Indeed, at his coronation, he stated that he would not wear his crown again until he had recovered the lands lost by his father.

Edward was a fighter, fierce and energetic, and beholden to the ideals of chivalry. He was on crusade when he inherited the throne, returning only two years later via a challenge in Châlons where he defeated a much larger force of French knights as well as gaining personal glory in individual combat. His was a fascinating clash of personalities. Harsh and domineering over men, yet gentle and loving with his wives and mother. Ambitious and greedy for territory, yet an enthusiastic moderniser of law and justice. Self-confident and a believer in the king's personal authority, yet willing to encourage the growth of a parliament to advise and govern alongside him.

Edward is not remembered fondly in either Wales or Scotland, having successfully annexed the former into the English realm and hammering the latter into a form of submission (though never completely conquering them.) Nor should his expulsion of the Jews from England be overlooked. His legacy however is undeniable. Our modern parliament, our codes of law, the castles at Beaumaris, Caernarfon and Harlech, the title 'Prince of Wales', the stone of Scone over which all subsequent English monarchs have been crowned, the memorial crosses for his beloved Eleanor at Waltham Cross and Charing Cross amongst others, the relative unity of England and Wales - owe much if not all to this powerful king.

In 1307 Edward was once more at war with the Scots, travelling north to fight Robert the Bruce. At 68 the six foot tall, snowy-haired Edward was already venerably old for his day. He had also been sickening for some time, probably of bowel cancer, possibly worsened by dysentery. At the Solway Firth near Burgh-by-Sands in Cumbria he stopped, feeling that he could go no further. He died shortly after, having stipulated that his bones were to be boiled and taken into every future battle against the Scots, and that his heart was to be taken to the Holy Land. Neither of these happened. Instead his body was laid out in St. Michael's church in Burgh before being carried to Westminster Abbey where he was buried alongside Eleanor.

The church bears no memorial to Edward, but it is a fascinating reminder of the troubles that this area suffered from marauding Scots. The tower is fortified, with no entrances at ground level. There is a wonderful statue of Edward further down the village, erected on the 700th anniversary of his death '07/07/07'.

In the salt marshes of Solway Firth near Burgh village there is a memorial in his honour, erected in 1685, rebuilt in 1803, and believed to mark the spot where Edward died. It can be reached easily by a footpath from the village centre, and is very well signposted. A visit to Burgh shows how important the 'Hammer of the Scots' was to the area, and just what an impact his death made. Without their fierce protector, Cumbria was open to the ravages of Robert the Bruce and generations of Scots to follow.

31. St. Michael's church, Burgh-by-Sands.

32. Memorial to Edward I at Burgh-by-Sands. The modern plaque reads 'Edward I fought a long and bitter campaign to conquer Scotland. Old and sick he made camp on these marshes whilst preparing to subdue his enemy Robert the Bruce. Edward died here on July 7 1307'.

Edward's tomb in Westminster Abbey is disappointing for such a great king. It is a plain, black, stone sarcophagus with no effigy, on the north side of the Shrine of St. Edward the Confessor. His nickname 'Hammer of the Scots' comes from some sixteenth-century graffiti on the tomb 'Edward primus Scottorum malleus hic est. Pactum serva'.

EDWARD II

    BORN 1284
    REIGNED FROM 1307 TO 1327
    DIED 21 SEPTEMBER 1327
    AT: BERKELEY CASTLE, GLOUCESTERSHIRE
    BURIED: GLOUCESTER CATHEDRAL

Edward II was as unlike his powerful father Edward I as it was possible to be. Though tall, handsome and intelligent, he was 'unkingly' in many ways. No natural warrior, he spent his youth rowing and riding chariots, and learning trades such as roofing and pit-digging. He loved music, art and plays, dedicating much time and money to elaborate productions for his court. Worst of all, to medieval minds, Edward was a homosexual, who showered his favourites with riches, titles and power, causing no end of resentment amongst an increasingly disillusioned and rebellious set of nobles.

His reign is notable for little except the resounding defeat to the Scots army of Robert the Bruce at Bannockburn, and for the manner of Edward's death. There had been a number of rebellions during his twenty years on the throne, all eventually put down, but the one that was to prove his undoing was led by his wife, Queen Isabella of France. Angered at being ignored by Edward in favour of first Piers Gaveston and then Hugh Despenser, and in league with her lover Mortimer the Earl of March, Isabella rallied England to her cause. Parliament formally deposed Edward in January 1327, and from that moment Isabella effectively ruled England through their son and Edward's successor, Edward III.

There is much that is uncertain about Edward II's last days. He was imprisoned in various castles, the last of which was Berkeley Castle in Gloucestershire. Here he was starved, left in a filthy state and thrown into a pit of rotting animal carcasses in the hope that he might die of 'natural' causes. When he failed to do so – he was a fit, healthy 43 year-old – Isabella is reputed to have ordered his murder, but by means such that there would be no external injury. It is said that Edward was held down by the weight of a heavy door whilst a horn was inserted into his anus, followed by a hot iron poker. The next day Edward was dead; his enemies may well have thought it was an appropriate punishment for a homosexual. Berkeley Castle is an outstanding place to visit, owned and lived in by the same family for some 900 years. The cell in which Edward was kept, and the pit where he and other prisoners were thrown, are in the King's Gallery in the Keep, the oldest part of the castle. The cell looks quite cosy now, but in Edward's time would have been a dark and cold place.

Many in England were horrified by his treatment at Berkeley Castle, among them his son, who sought later to ease his conscience at his involvement in his overthrow by building a fine effigy at his tomb and trying to restore his father's reputation. There were indeed pilgrimages made to his tomb, and fruitless attempts at canonisation of a supposed martyr who was believed to perform posthumous miracles.

Edward was buried on the north side of the quire in the abbey church of St. Peter in Gloucester, which after the reformation became Gloucester Cathedral (and was not left to ruin like so many abbeys partly because it housed the remains of a king). The revenues from the pilgrims to his shrine helped to finance the construction work in the church, which took several years. The alabaster, limestone and Purbeck marble shrine is one of the finest of any English king, indeed of any public figure, an undeserved monument to a pathetic monarch.

33. Berkeley Castle, Gloucestershire.

34. Gloucester Cathedral from the centre of the cloisters. Edward II's tomb was closed for restoration at the time of writing. See front cover for a photograph of the upper part of Edward's effigy.

EDWARD III

   🔔   BORN 1312
   ✠   REIGNED FROM 1327 TO 1377
   ✝   DIED 22 JUNE 1377
       AT: SHEEN PALACE (LATER RICHMOND PALACE), SURREY
       BURIED: WESTMINSTER ABBEY

Edward III's reign was a long one – fifty years – with a striking contrast between first and second halves. His rule reads like a schoolboy's history book: the Hundred Years War, the Black Death, the Order of the Garter, the Black Prince. Edward was tall and handsome with reddish-blond hair and was an archetypal medieval king, in turn chivalrous, warlike, aloof, loving, despotic and glamorous. Even if he hadn't rescued the monarchy from the disaster that was Edward II's reign and from the clutches of the power-hungry Mortimer and Isabella, he would have been hugely popular throughout England. Edward had a way about him that just proclaimed 'Majesty'.

Edward's reign began with an anomaly, something unprecedented, at least since some time before William the Conqueror. Edward, at the age of just 14, was crowned while the previous incumbent was still alive. Just four years later Edward showed his character by seizing full control of his realm, executing his grasping regent Mortimer and imprisoning his mother Isabella for life. The next fifteen years or so saw Edward build a stunning tomb effigy for his father in Gloucester as an act of penitence, subdue the Scots, declare himself rightful King of France (thus starting the Hundred Years War), experiment with innovative military strategy, and win a great battle against the French at Crécy. His happy and fruitful marriage to Philippa of Hainault lasted 30 years, bringing with it good counsel and a useful counterbalance to Edward's sometimes overly-enthusiastic approach to kingship.

From 1348 however things started going wrong. The Black Death hit Europe hard, killing about one third of the population, and putting a temporary end to Edward's warmongering in France. His relations with Parliament were never easy, but between them they managed the aftermath of the plague remarkably well, bringing in radical new statutes to control prices and wages. Soon he was off to war with France again, his eldest son the Black Prince covering himself with glory at the Battle of Poitiers, and gaining much territory. Further years of war saw Edward on the very point of claiming the French crown, but rebellion in Aquitaine and a revitalised French campaign under their new King Charles V pushed the English back. Edward eventually lost most of his conquests, the Black Prince and Philippa died, and the king became more and more detached, falling into the hands of a greedy mistress.

His final months were passed, incapacitated and virtually alone, in the Palace at Sheen (now Richmond, Surrey). It was here that Edward died, his mistress Alice Perrers reputedly stripping the rings from his fingers before his body was cold. Little remains of the once highly-favoured Richmond Palace, and nothing of the original medieval buildings, but a visit to Richmond is worthwhile to see the Tudor remains. (See also Henry VII)

Edward was buried amidst much public mourning in Westminster Abbey alongside his wife Philippa. The inscription on his tomb can be translated as 'Here is the glory of the English, the paragon of past kings, the model of future kings, a merciful king, the peace of the peoples, Edward the Third fulfilling the jubilee of his reign, the unconquered leopard, powerful in war like a Maccabee. While he lived prosperously, his realm lived again in honesty. He ruled mighty in arms; now in Heaven let him be a king' (translation source: Westminster Abbey website).

35. One of many reminders in Richmond of the great palace that once stood here.

36. Side view of Edward III's tomb and effigy at Westminster.

RICHARD II

⌂ BORN 1367
✠ REIGNED FROM 1377 TO 1399
✟ DIED 14 FEBRUARY 1400
AT: PONTEFRACT CASTLE, YORKSHIRE
BURIED: KING'S LANGLEY, HERTFORDSHIRE THEN WESTMINSTER ABBEY

Whilst a king who inherits his crown as a child always faces problems, Richard II's were mostly of his own making. At his accession the monarchy was in a relatively healthy state. His grandfather Edward III had for the most part been a strong, popular king and had done his best to ensure the magnates accepted the ten-year old Richard as their next king. Importantly, the young boy had the loyal support of his powerful uncle John of Gaunt. Richard's father was the heroic Black Prince, eldest son of Edward III, who should of course have been crowned king had he not died of illness just a year previously. Such illustrious parentage provided Richard with many staunch allies. Furthermore at the age of fourteen Richard won admiration for his personal bravery in repressing the Peasants Revolt, and for his savagery in punishing the ringleaders afterwards. His treachery and brutality were seen as signs of good kingship, very much a mark of the times.

After this show of strength Richard's true character came to the fore. He was vain, arrogant, deceitful and quick-tempered, and ruled over an immoral, lascivious court. Like Edward II he had favourites who caused much resentment amongst the nobility, and like Edward he was rumoured to be homosexual. With his complete disdain for war and for personal valour, and his increasing

37. Richard is believed to have been killed in the Gascoigne Tower, the arched ruin just visible to the right of the keep.

38. Richard II was originally buried in the priory church near this, the only remaining medieval monastic building.

interest in the occult, he soon lost respect both as an individual and as a king. Further outbreaks of plague, a particularly harsh famine in 1391, and an inability to produce an heir further undermined Richard's position.

Then, in early 1399, John of Gaunt died. Rich, highly respected and in charge of much of the army, John had in reality been the only thing between Richard and an even earlier demise. However it was surprising just how quickly Richard's position crumbled. John's son (and Richard's first cousin) Henry Bolingbroke, came back from exile to enforce his claim to the throne. Richard was captured and imprisoned, first in Conway Castle and finally in Pontefract Castle in Henry's heartland. Henry's grasp on the crown was weak and he certainly could not afford to let his enemies gather around his predecessor's cause. Although Richard had officially abdicated, or been forced to by Parliament, Henry wanted to prove that Richard had actually died of natural causes, and to display his dead body to stifle rumours of a comeback. It was therefore in Pontefract Castle that Richard met his end.

Many believe that Richard was starved to death or smothered, but this is inconsistent with a report that he fell ill in early February 1400 and took some ten days to die. Much more likely is that he was poisoned. Pontefract Castle was once one of the largest in the country, an impressive bastion of the House of Lancaster. It is now a well tended but rather sad ruin, lacking its former grandeur and ability to induce terror. Richard is supposed to have been killed in the Gascoigne Tower, just to the right of the keep. It is well signposted.

Henry took great care to pay due respects to the dead king, thus emphasising both Richard's demise and his own rightful succession. After being displayed in St. Paul's Cathedral in London, Richard's body was buried in the somewhat obscure priory church of the Dominican Friars at King's Langley, Hertfordshire. Although this church was next to a royal palace (since demolished) and there were a couple of royal tombs in the area, it was not Richard's stated choice of

Westminster Abbey but rather 'out of sight, out of mind'. All that remains now of the monastic buildings is the prior's house, in a rather sad state in the private grounds of a school.

Richard was later re-interred in Westminster Abbey by a conscience-stricken Henry V who had formed a close bond with his late cousin whilst travelling as a hostage with him in Ireland. Henry also wanted to strengthen his own hold on the throne by stressing the fact that Richard was truly dead, following persistent rumours to the contrary. Well before his abdication Richard II had ordered the construction of his own tomb in Westminster Abbey so that he could rest in perpetuity next to his much-loved queen, Anne. Henry V moved his body from King's Langley to its final resting place near the Shrine of Edward the Confessor in the abbey in 1413. The tomb effigy, in gilt bronze, is one of the most beautiful of any English monarch, rich in Plantagenet decoration, and easily viewed from inside the chapel.

HENRY IV

⏣ Born 1367

✠ Reigned from 1399 to 1413

♱ Died 21 March 1413

    At: Westminster Abbey

    Buried: Canterbury Cathedral

The great usurper Henry IV brought the house of Lancaster to the throne, sowing the seeds of the Wars of the Roses. Henry and Richard, his predecessor and first cousin, grew up together but whereas Richard was effete, sensitive and all too aware of his kingly inheritance, Henry was combative, tough and ambitious in only one thing – to be a champion knight. Much of his early life was spent jousting, winning prestigious tournaments and crusading. He covered himself in glory by joining the Teutonic knights to rid Lithuania of its pagan rulers, and was the only English king to have visited Jerusalem, albeit in a peaceable context. Henry was athletic, strong, handsome and able to hold his own with the intellectuals of the day.

However, he really shouldn't have become king. This fact haunted him and his Lancastrian heirs throughout their reigns. Henry was the son of John of Gaunt, only the third son of Edward III, and there were others with stronger legal rights to the crown. For many years Richard had been wary of Henry, and took the first opportunity, when John of Gaunt died, to banish Henry to France and strip him of his assets and titles. In 1399 Henry returned to England to reclaim what he believed was rightfully his. It seems that at this point that was all he wanted – he may not have had ambitions for the throne. However Richard was hugely unpopular, he was away in Ireland, and all his supporters flocked to the young and dashing champion Henry. Very soon he had his eye on the ultimate prize. The king's forced abdication, his murder (probably upon Henry's direct orders) and Parliament's reluctant acceptance of Henry's claim to the throne by force of arms, all followed rapidly.

The rest of Henry's fourteen years were spent battling rebels, the Welsh and disease. Almost continuously, different factions rose up against him, supporting the claim of yet another of Edward III's descendants, and even of the dead Richard II who was believed to be alive still. Some of Henry's staunchest allies turned against him. The Percies of Northumberland led by Harry Hotspur allied themselves with Owen Glendower and the Scots, losing one of England's bloodiest battles to Henry at Shrewsbury in 1403. After one rebellion Henry had the Archbishop of York executed, much to everybody's horror. From that day onwards Henry suffered from an irritating, itchy skin disease, and believed it to be a curse from God. He started suffering from fits, grew more and more reclusive, and increasingly resentful of his son, the future Henry V, who began to rule on his behalf.

The end came as Henry was preparing to go on crusade to the Holy Land, for a prophecy had told him he would die in Jerusalem. He fainted whilst praying in Westminster Abbey, and was moved to a small room to recover. On regaining consciousness Henry asked where he was, to which the reply came 'the Jerusalem Chamber'. Thus the prophecy was fulfilled, and Henry died, a forlorn shadow of his former glorious figure. The Jerusalem Chamber is now a part of the Deanery of Westminster Abbey, and can be seen jutting out of the west side by the great door, next to the bookshop. It is a place of work and not open to the general public. Inside a bust of Henry IV commemorates the association.

His wish to be buried in Canterbury Cathedral was probably because there was little room near the shrine of Edward the Confessor in Westminster Abbey, rather than because he had a burning desire to be in Canterbury. Many see it as ironic that the killer of an archbishop should be buried

39. The outside of the Jerusalem Chamber in Westminster Abbey, where Henry IV died. The arched doorway is the main west exit/entrance.

40. Henry IV is the only monarch to be buried in Canterbury Cathedral, although the Black Prince's tomb is only a few metres away.

so close to the shrine of another archbishop killed by a former king – Thomas à Becket was slain by Henry II's men nearby. It is also ironic that he should be buried opposite the Black Prince, whose son he usurped.

Henry's tomb is one of the most magnificent in England. On the south side of the quire, his canopy is painted in blue, gold and red, and supported by pious figures bearing shields. The effigies of Henry and his queen, Joan, are of alabaster, decorated generously. Although they are surrounded by an old iron railing, the Cathedral authorities have provided steps so you can climb above this and examine the recumbent figures very closely.

HENRY V

🔔 BORN 1387
✠ REIGNED FROM 1413 TO 1422
✝ DIED 31 AUGUST 1422
AT: CHATEAU DE VINCENNES, VAL-DE-MARNE, FRANCE
BURIED: WESTMINSTER ABBEY; ENTRAILS IN SAINT-MAUR-DES-FOSSÉS, VAL-DE-MARNE, FRANCE

'And Crispin Crispian shall ne'er go by,
From this day to the ending of the world
But we in it shall be remembered,-
We few, we happy few, we band of brothers;'
(*King Henry The Fifth*, William Shakespeare)

It is very difficult to get past the heroic, shakespearian image we all have of Henry V. His legend has grown such that he is regarded today as the greatest of our medieval kings, a resounding example of 'Englishness', endowed with fighting spirit, chivalry, resilience and majesty – almost everything a good English king should have.

And of course Shakespeare superbly captured much of Henry's character. The quotation above from Act IV Scene III illustrates both his stirring qualities as a leader of men-at-war and his burning ambition to be remembered as a great king through posterity, traits which few modern historians question. What is more debatable, in terms of understanding Henry fully, is his maltreatment of former friends, his acts of barbarity and his subjugation of England's interests to his own. As a young man Henry was a womanising, carousing practical joker who also displayed supreme skill and toughness campaigning against both Irish and Welsh insurgents. He was shot in the face by an arrow at the bloody Battle of Shrewsbury but did not leave the battlefield. He was highly ambitious, incurring the wrath and deep suspicion of his ailing father, Henry IV. However, when Henry became king he seemed to change, almost overnight. He became a pious, serious man who renounced all his former activities and devoted himself to carrying war to the French, and eventually he hoped, to the Holy Land.

He executed an old friend for reportedly being a member of a heretical religious sect, the lollards. He did not hesitate to order the massacre of his noblemen prisoners at Agincourt, against every code of honour, when he thought they might pose a threat towards the end of the battle. He bled English coffers to finance his dream of uniting the English and French crowns; a dream that he came nearer to fulfilling than any other English monarch. He inflicted ever more savage punishment on his soldiers for disobeying orders. Yet, his people and his army loved him. The celebrations after his successes in France were unsurpassed, and along with Edward III he was perhaps most responsible for the birth of England as a great and influential European power. The revisionist historians are fighting a losing battle. In everyman's hearts it will always be 'Cry, God for Harry! England and Saint George!' (Act III Scene I)

Henry died in August 1422 whilst on campaign in France, just one month before the French king whose crown he would have inherited. Nine years of campaigning and bearing the responsibilities of kingship had worn him down. He succumbed to dysentery, possibly worsened by a cancer or other illness of the rectum. He bid farewell to his young wife Katherine of Valois from his sickbed in his headquarters in the Chateau de Vincennes near Paris, but he never saw his son, born just after he left for France. The chateau is the only surviving medieval royal residence in France, and has been beautifully restored. Henry most likely died in the royal bedchamber on the second floor

41. Chateau de Vincennes, on the outskirts of Paris.

42. The ruined abbey in Saint-Maur-des-Fossés.

43. Henry V's chantry overlooking the shrine of Edward the Confessor in Westminster Abbey. The sarcophagus is behind the iron gate.

of the keep, which retains original paintwork, wooden wall-hangings and stone carvings, but may have died in the old royal manor in the courtyard, which has since disappeared.

After death his body was cut up, the flesh boiled off, and the bones laid in state in the church of St. Denis. The liquid was poured onto the ground near the church, and the viscera buried in the grounds of the Abbey of Saint-Maur-des-Fossés on the outskirts of Paris. At the time this was a very important foundation, and a great centre of pilgrimage. The abbey is little more than a ruin today, but sits in a neat little park with good map boards showing the original layout. Henry's innards were buried in the cemetery just in front of the ruined pillar in the photo. There is no memorial.

His bones were sent to Westminster Abbey for internment, where he still lies in close proximity to the central shrine of Edward the Confessor, behind a magnificent chantry, reflecting how much he was revered.

HENRY VI

⚜ BORN 1421

✠ REIGNED FROM 1422 TO 1461 AND 1470 TO 1471

✟ DIED 21 MAY 1471

AT: TOWER OF LONDON

BURIED: CHERTSEY ABBEY THEN ST. GEORGE'S CHAPEL, WINDSOR

Henry VI is remembered today as the founder of Eton College and of King's College Cambridge, and as the subject of a Shakespeare play. He is also the only English king to inherit the throne whilst under the age of one, and the only English king to be crowned King of France. Henry was pious, serious, high-minded, generous, friendly and forgiving – in sum, a good man. But these characteristics do not make for a good king, and in the swirling, devious, power-hungry atmosphere that was fifteenth-century politics, he was utterly lost. Henry was to inherit two realms and to lose them both. Indeed, he lost the English one twice.

His antipathy to being king aside, Henry had the misfortune both to gain the crown at nine months old and to be the subject of a disputed inheritance (his grandfather, the Lancastrian Henry IV, had usurped the crown). There were plenty of powerful men whose claims to be descended from a higher source than the third son of Edward III were causes justes for rebellions. Henry, though undoubtedly a worthy fellow, fostered no respect from his nobles who wanted an assertive, commanding king such as his father Henry V. He progressively lost all the French land that his father had gained, except Calais, as the French, inspired by Joan of Arc, rallied around their new king Charles VII. His court was ruined by favouritism, not helped by his marriage to the forceful Margaret of Anjou. Henry also suffered from a series of psychotic traumas, unable to recognise his infant son at times, let alone rule.

The power struggle eventually burst into armed conflict, what we now call the Wars of the Roses. Henry became a pawn, dragged from castle to castle, sometimes imprisoned by the Yorkists, sometimes the figurehead of an army raised by Margaret to defend their son's inheritance. In 1461 Edward of York seized the crown and Henry was imprisoned in the Tower of London, where he was maltreated and abused, but for nine years was probably happier leading a monk's existence than a king's. Then in 1470 Margaret and the Earl of Warwick managed to overthrow the Yorkist Edward, and Henry was re-installed as a puppet king for a year. Edward however returned, defeated the Lancastrian forces, and imprisoned Henry once more in the Tower.

To consolidate his position, Edward decided to annihilate the Lancastrian line, and had Henry murdered. It is not known exactly how he was killed or who did it, but you can visit the Wakefield Tower in the Tower of London where he is supposed to have met his end.

His body was embalmed and put on display to avoid any doubt that he was indeed dead. Edward had him buried in the obscure Chertsey Abbey, but he became almost more powerful in death than in life, acquiring a reputation as a martyr and a saint. Miracles at his tomb were recognised by the Pope. Edward certainly hadn't foreseen this! Today Chertsey is a pleasant town, but it is a real pity that so little remains of the abbey and of Henry's original burial place. There are a few walls and a memorial plaque in Abbey Gardens, and a few other scattered structures, mostly re-built incorporating old abbey stone.

Richard III had his body re-interred at Windsor to suppress the growing cult of Henry the martyr. Henry VII nearly succeeded in having his Lancastrian predecessor canonised. It was only the latter's death, and the subsequent divorce of the Church of England from Roman Catholicism under Henry VIII that put paid to a second saintly King of England. Henry's tomb in St. George's Chapel is marked by a very simple black stone slab, inscribed 'Henry VI' and with his seal. It was erected as late as 1790 but moved to directly above his vault in the twentieth century. You can find it to the west side of Edward VII's monument, and somewhat ironically, nearly opposite the great chantry of his nemesis Edward IV.

44. Wakefield Tower where Henry is alleged to have been murdered.

45. Little remains of Chertsey Abbey except a few stunted, ruined or re-built walls.

46. St. George's Chapel, Windsor, from the south.

EDWARD IV

   ⌂   BORN 1442
   ✠   REIGNED FROM 1461 TO 1470 AND 1471 TO 1483
   ✝   DIED 9 APRIL 1483
        AT: PALACE OF WESTMINSTER
        BURIED: ST. GEORGE'S CHAPEL, WINDSOR

At 6'4" Edward IV was England's tallest monarch, and reputedly one of the most handsome. He had a nearly insatiable appetite for drinking and sex, comfortable in the company of peasants and dukes, whores and countesses. Medieval England did not hold this against him – indeed they took it as a positive – for Edward was everything that his rival and predecessor wasn't. He was warlike, a master strategist, commanding, ambitious as well as being lively and fun. And although merry-making and money-making were his two passions, he was just enough in control of his senses and of his advisors to rule England effectively. Happy to let the Earl of Warwick, his chief minister, get on with running the country, Edward knew when to step in and sanction important decisions.

Edward was the first Yorkist king, being the son of Richard of York, and tracing his lineage back to Edmund, another of Edward III's sons. His claim to the throne was perhaps even weaker than that of Henry VI (who was related to John of Gaunt, Duke of Lancaster, an older son of Edward III) but legal rights had been overshadowed by force majeur at this stage. Some very bloody battles settled the succession, although Edward suffered a temporary setback when he was forced to flee the country in 1470, as Henry VI returned as king under the turncoat and all-controlling Earl of Warwick. Edward's personality won him back the throne in 1471 as people flooded back to him from the dull, unkingly Henry.

The second half of his reign was a relatively peaceful, prosperous time and Edward was able to indulge his weaknesses. Despite years of self-abuse and a tendency to fatness, it was still a great surprise when he succumbed to a chill from fishing on the Thames in winter at the age of just 40. England genuinely mourned their loss. Edward's legacy though is paltry. Perhaps because he is sandwiched between such notable Shakespearian heroes and antiheroes, and perhaps because his time is indelibly associated with the horrors of the Wars of the Roses, he is not well known today. His greatest monument is St. George's Chapel in Windsor Castle which he had built to outdo Henry VI's efforts at Eton and Cambridge, and into which he poured considerable direction and money. Edward died in one of his chambers at the Palace of Westminster. Nothing survives of the medieval palace which burnt down in the 1830s, except the Great Hall, which is visible from the road but visitable only with a special tour, often arranged through an MP. It is well worth seeing.

After lying in state for a number of days he was buried in his new chapel at Windsor. An elaborate monument was planned, but instead we have just a slab of black marble marking his vault to the north side of the high altar. Another black marble slab was erected on the wall above in the late eighteenth century, inscribed 'Edward IIIJ'. However on the other side of this memorial, and overlooking the altar itself, is a superb chantry and a set of highly intricate iron gates. The beautiful, ornate window above the gates was built by Henry VIII for Catherine of Aragon, but the stone window to the left is original. The tomb was interfered with at some stage, but in the main escaped damage during the civil war.

Above: 47. The Palace of Westminster. The medieval Great Hall built by William II can be seen behind the outer wall, behind the statue of Oliver Cromwell.

Right: 48. Edward IV's chantry and iron gates, St. George's Chapel, Windsor.

EDWARD V – ONE OF THE 'PRINCES IN THE TOWER'

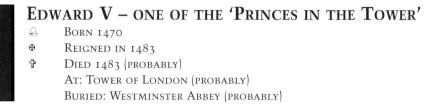

   BORN 1470
   REIGNED IN 1483
   DIED 1483 (PROBABLY)
   AT: TOWER OF LONDON (PROBABLY)
   BURIED: WESTMINSTER ABBEY (PROBABLY)

Edward V suffered one of the shortest reigns of any English monarch. As eldest son of Edward IV he was the rightful heir to the throne and showed much youthful promise. His father died unexpectedly at the age of 40 but had taken precautions with his magnates to confirm they would recognise the 13 year old Edward as the next king. Edward IV's loyal brother Richard was amongst these noblemen swearing fealty.

Unfortunately Richard hated the young Edward's mother, Elizabeth Woodville, a grasping, scheming commoner who had had a hand in the earlier execution of another of Richard's brothers. Fearing his own exclusion from power, Richard rushed to take control soon after Edward IV's death, by capturing Edward V on his journey to London and executing as many Woodvilles as possible. At some stage he decided to seize the throne himself, turning from officially recognised 'Protector' to the man that Parliament officially proclaimed king. To avoid rival factions gaining a hold, Edward V had to disappear.

During these weeks of power-struggle, Edward V and his nine year old brother Richard had been quartered in the Tower of London. They were observed playing in the gardens, and were

49. The White Tower, Tower of London, possible original burial site of Edward V.

50. The Bloody Tower, Tower of London, where Edward and his brother are believed to have been murdered.

attended by a number of nurses and physicians. Over a short period of time sightings of the two boys became more and more infrequent until one day they disappeared altogether. No one can be sure what happened to them, or where they are buried, but the mystery of the 'Princes in the Tower' is poignant, and infamous even today. In the seventeenth century workmen demolishing a staircase in the White Tower came across a wooden chest containing the skeletons of two children.

In the White Tower, on the way up to the entrance, you can see the staircase and a descriptive plaque, together with a romanticised picture of the foul murder.

The bones have never been categorically identified as the two princes, but Charles II had them re-buried in an urn in the north aisle of Henry VII's Lady Chapel in Westminster Abbey, now known as Innocents' Corner after the children commemorated there. The inscription can be translated as:

'Here lie the relics of Edward V, King of England, and Richard, Duke of York. These brothers being confined in the Tower of London, and there stifled with pillows, were privately and meanly buried, by the order of their perfidious uncle Richard the Usurper; whose bones, long enquired after and wished for, after 191 years in the rubbish of the stairs (those lately leading to the Chapel of the White Tower) were on the 17th day of July 1674, by undoubted proofs discovered, being buried deep in that place. Charles II, a most compassionate prince, pitying their severe fate, ordered these unhappy Princes to be laid amongst the monuments of their predecessors, 1678, in the 30th year of his reign' (Source: The Westminster Abbey website)

51. A Victorian memorial plaque to Edward V in the White Tower.

52. The sarcophagus designed by Sir Christopher Wren to house the urn in Westminster Abbey.

RICHARD III

⌂ BORN 1452

✠ REIGNED FROM 1483 TO 1485

♱ DIED 22 AUGUST 1485

AT: BOSWORTH FIELD, LEICESTERSHIRE

BURIED: GREY FRIARS CHURCH, LEICESTER THEN POSSIBLY LOST

Richard III, despite his short reign, is one of our most fascinating kings. He was born the eleventh child of Richard, Duke of York, barely expected to survive a sickly childhood let alone rise to the throne of England. He was staunchly loyal to his brother Edward IV, disdaining life at court because of his antipathy to Edward's wife, but governing the north of the country well from his base in Yorkshire and keeping marauding Scots in check. He was certainly no hunchback – a myth perpetuated by Shakespeare to further malign the Yorkist king who had been deposed by the predecessors of Shakespeare's paymasters – though he did suffer from a sideways curvature of the spine. And he was a courageous, warrior king who died leading a fearless horseback charge at his rival at the battle of Bosworth.

We shouldn't glamorise Richard too much though. Loyal as he was up to 1483, after Edward IV's death he lost little time in questioning his brother's legitimacy and usurping Edward's son, the newly proclaimed Edward V. No one has proved that Richard murdered the young Edward V and his brother, but they disappeared from the Tower of London at some stage and were never seen again. Richard clearly saw an opportunity for power and grabbed it, or maybe feared that if he did not do so, he would in turn be ousted from his favourable position by his hated in-laws. Maybe it was Hobson's choice, but once made, Richard sat uneasily on his throne and it was necessary to get rid of rivals. His personal reputation irreparably damaged and his tenure of the crown questionable, rebellion was rife. His three year reign was spent executing former allies who turned against him, and those whom Richard suspected of doing so.

Richard's last battle at Bosworth has given rise to much folklore. The precise location of the battlefield is unknown, his crown is alleged to have been retrieved from a hawthorn bush and placed on the head of the victorious Henry Tudor, and the treachery and calculated indecision of several participants is legendary. This was the last time an English monarch would fall in pitched battle, heroically cut down by Henry's household guards, and indeed the only one since Harold. Richard has been the subject of much vilification and subsequent reappraisal over the years; in reality he would have made a good king but made some injudicious (and immoral) decisions which led to his early demise, and to the end of the Plantagenet line.

Finding either the spot where he died or where he is buried is nigh impossible. Finding proxies for either is relatively straightforward. The site of the battle of Bosworth is the subject of several theories. The most commonly accepted is that by Ambion Hill where there is an excellent visitor centre and a trail around the assumed battlefield. At the time of writing, extensive research is casting new light on the whereabouts of key events and participants. For now, it is most likely that Richard and his banner were at the top of Ambion Hill before the battle, owning the high ground, looking westwards to the approaching Henry.

There is also a monument recording where Richard fell, near the stream where he valiantly attacked Henry and his bodyguards. This is almost certainly in the wrong place, but is treasured by modern-day supporters of Richard and therefore unlikely to be moved. It can be seen to the northwest of the battlefield trail, near the railway bridge.

After the battle we know that Richard's body was stripped, carried on horseback to nearby Leicester, and displayed for all to see that the usurper was dead. It is most likely that he was then

53. View over the site of the battle of Bosworth from Richard's standard, but subject to much conjecture.

54. Monument purporting to show where Richard died in glorious failure, trying to kill Henry Tudor and thus clinch instant victory, on the field of the battle of Bosworth.

Above: 55. One of the buildings at the St. Martin's end of Grey Friars Street, Leicester, probable burial site of Richard III.

Right: 56. Plaque marking Richard III's legendary, final resting place by the river.

buried in the friary church of the Franciscan order in Leicester, commonly called the Grey Friars Church. His successor Henry VII commissioned a tomb for him, but church, tomb and graveyard fell victim to the Reformation and were demolished, being built upon several times until the twentieth century. Little remains of the church bar a few stones in a wall and an underground arch. It is quite probable that Richard lies buried beneath one of the buildings now on the site of the church choir, but the exact location of even this is uncertain. Some excellent research has been done by the Richard III Foundation, available online in the Leicester Chronicler, but it is impossible to be conclusive.

There is also a legend that Richard's bones were disinterred by a mob during the Reformation and thrown into the River Soar by Bow Bridge. Many bones have been found, many theories abound, few if any are likely to be correct. There is a plaque commemorating Richard's supposed final resting place, on a wall by the iron bridge that replaced the old medieval stone one. Originally inscribed in 1861 by a local builder, it is in a somewhat shabby location, and does little to evoke the famous prediction of an old woman in 1485, who foretold that on his return from battle, Richard's head would strike the spot on the bridge where his spur had struck on his way out.

HENRY VII

△ BORN 1457

✠ REIGNED FROM 1485 TO 1509

✞ DIED 21 APRIL 1509

AT: RICHMOND PALACE, SURREY

BURIED: WESTMINSTER ABBEY

There are few kings as understated as Henry VII, overshadowed as he is by his son Henry VIII. Yet Henry revolutionised the monarchy and turned England around. Yes, he was a dull, prudent king, but that was just what the country needed. His marriage to Elizabeth of York re-united Lancastrian and Yorkist dynasties, ending years of war and strife. He established the Tudor line whose subsequent monarchs would bring unimaginable glories to the nation. His common sense and financial awareness brought a level of governance barely seen in Europe at that time. Moreover he sponsored John Cabot's adventures in Canada, bringing England into the race for domination in overseas trade and empire-building.

Little of this seemed probable when Henry was born in 1457, son of Edmund Tudor, Earl of Richmond. Various murders, executions and deaths in battle led to Henry becoming head of the Lancastrian cause and more importantly the senior male descendant of Edward III's son John of Gaunt – with a higher legal claim to the throne than both Edward IV and Richard III, descendants of a younger son Edmund. Henry's early years were shaped by the ups and downs of the Lancastrian family and by many years in exile, almost as a hostage, in Brittany. He was an intelligent, well-educated man and not at all a warrior, most unusual for that period. He also had the good fortune to strike against Richard III at a time when the king's popularity was at a low, and to carry the day at Bosworth against a vastly more battle-hardened foe.

His early years as king were marked by several rebellions, two of which centred around commoners pretending to be long-lost royals. All were successfully suppressed. Henry's ability in controlling the magnates, his good sense and the lavish dress and feasts at court all helped to increase his popularity with a nation tired of war. Trade and judicious taxes swelled Henry's own coffers and those of his landowners. The Tudor inheritance was firmly established by the turn of the century, at which point Henry's life started to crumble. His beloved wife and four of his five children died, he began to suffer from a debilitating illness and he became more and more reclusive and argumentative, sometimes striking his surviving son and heir Henry.

Henry VII finally died of tuberculosis at his treasured Richmond Palace. Originally called Sheen Palace, Henry had it rebuilt in 1501 and renamed after his earldom. It was a beautiful building, and was the favourite of a number of later monarchs including Henry VIII and Elizabeth I. All the more shame that so little exists today. A number of the Tudor buildings that escaped destruction and redevelopment can be seen, although a few are hidden in a private estate; there is an excellent site map on the green in front of the gateway (see also Elizabeth I).

One of Henry's most impressive legacies is his chapel and tomb at Westminster Abbey. His Lady Chapel is a stunning construction in English Perpendicular style with a delicate fan vaulted roof, surrounded by Tudor emblems, and in total contrast to the rest of the abbey. It has been called 'one of the most perfect buildings ever erected in England'. His tomb is magnificent also, depicting Henry and his wife in bronze-gilt, recumbent in prayer above a black marble tomb. The intricate brass screen surrounding it is perhaps one reason why it is in such fine condition. Henry's coffin is in a vault beneath the tomb.

In the **1740s**, the 3rd Earl of Cholmondeley built a house on this site.

In **1780**, the house was bought and enlarged by the
4th Duke of Queensberry who entertained here in grand style.
The Prince Regent was a frequent visitor.

In **1830** Sir William Dundas built the next Queensberry House
which survived until **1933** when the present flats replaced it.

This history was researched by Roy Price CB (1916-2005) a resident here.

Above: 57. A plaque
on a modern house
commemorating the once
famous Richmond Palace.

Right: 58. Henry VII's
and Elizabeth's tomb
effigies.

HENRY VIII 'BLUFF KING HAL'

⚲ BORN 1491

✠ REIGNED FROM 1509 TO 1547

♱ DIED 28 JANUARY 1547

AT: WHITEHALL PALACE

BURIED: ST. GEORGE'S CHAPEL, WINDSOR

From exuberant, affable, deeply religious and athletic youth to ill-tempered, obese and self-centred monster in nearly four decades on the throne, Henry VIII almost defies the legend that has grown up around him. Remembered today primarily for having six wives and for splitting from the Roman Catholic church, Henry is a fascinating character, ruling at a time when England really began to shine as a world power.

The young Henry was a paragon of kings. He was exceedingly well-read, composed music in the new and complex polyphony that was developing at the time, jousted with the very best of knights, worshipped his queen Catherine of Aragon and ruled through a network of powerful, intelligent men such as Cardinal Wolsey. Henry seemed to let others rule his country for him, but they were under no deception – Henry had the ultimate say in any important matter. England prospered, became more and more wealthy, formed meaningful alliances with continental kings and emperors and finally rid itself of the continual rebellions and counter-claims for the throne (those of a serious nature in any event) that had plagued it for over a hundred years.

Henry seemed to have it all, and to enjoy it all too. So how did it all go wrong? First and foremost was the problem of succession. Catherine had only produced a daughter, and a female heir was unacceptable both to Henry, who feared for the continuation of the Tudor line, and to the magnates who feared a return to the civil war that occurred the previous time a woman was the natural successor, back in the twelfth century. This, and Henry's infatuation with the young Anne Boleyn, led to divorce, separation from the Catholic Church, the establishment of Protestantism and the dissolution of the monasteries. Its impact on England's development, now outside the family of European Catholic states, is hard to overstate. From then on Henry became more and more obsessed with siring a legitimate male heir, beheading or divorcing unfruitful or unsatisfactory queens. He became ever more convinced in his own decision-making, alienating and indeed executing many former friends who disagreed with him. Agonising illnesses, possibly even syphilis but certainly oozing leg ulcers and fevers, and gross obesity coupled with violent fits of temper made Henry almost unbearable to be with.

It was a relief to his courtiers that Henry finally passed away in January 1547 at his palace in Whitehall. This palace had become a favourite with Henry, who had expanded it considerably, partly through annexing Cardinal Wolsley's properties in 1530. Two disastrous fires in the 1690s, much development of townhouses, and the expansion of twentieth-century government buildings in the area mean that very few of the Tudor buildings are left to see today. This is a great shame as Whitehall Palace was the largest in Europe in its time and full of treasures. The modern sweep of Whitehall is somewhat grand but lacking any 'royal' feel.

Henry's huge carcass had to be lifted into an oversize coffin and carried to Windsor, via a lying-in-state at Syon House. Surprisingly there is no grand monument in St. George's Chapel to one of our most famous kings. Instead there is a simple stone slab near the centre of the quire, dating from 1837 with Henry's name in brass lettering, alongside the names of Jane Seymour, Charles I and one of Queen Anne's infants.

Above: 59. A modern view of Whitehall, mostly dating from the eighteenth to twentieth centuries.

Right: 60. The commemorative slab to Henry VIII in St. George's Chapel.

61. Greenwich as it is today. The stone slab commemorating the Tudor palace is in the foreground.

ON THIS SITE STOOD THE TUDOR PALACE OF GREENWICH BUILT BY KING HENRY VII

BIRTHPLACE
OF
KING HENRY VIII
IN 1491
AND HIS DAUGHTERS
QUEEN MARY I IN 1516
AND
QUEEN ELIZABETH I
IN 1533

62. Much archaeological digging was done in the 1970s in the area around this stone, to find out more about the lost palace.

EDWARD VI

⚐ BORN 1537
✠ REIGNED FROM 1547 TO 1553
♰ DIED 6 JULY 1553
AT: GREENWICH PALACE
BURIED: WESTMINSTER ABBEY

Poor Edward. So eagerly anticipated, Henry VIII's first and only legitimate son had a short and miserable life. Never has the flower of royal expectation withered so pitifully. Edward's mother died just eleven days after his birth, his father when he was but nine years old. He was born strong and healthy, but despite being wrapped in cotton wool and kept far from plague-infested London, his health deteriorated severely so that he grew into a pale, delicate youth, with spindly legs and one shoulder higher than the other. His increasingly irascible and temperamental father left him a clutch of tormented and power-hungry advisors who tried to outmanoeuvre each other to hold sway over the young successor. Edward also inherited a country battling itself over issues of faith and religion, where Protestantism was still poorly defined, centres of monastic learning had been overthrown and clergy were openly attacked in the streets.

Edward never had a chance to assert himself. The real power lay with first Edward Seymour, then with John Dudley, both of whom exercised executive control without taking into account any of the young king's wishes. King Edward was obviously frustrated, wanting to rule but lacking both knowledge and authority. At one stage he is said to have plucked his favourite falcon of all its feathers and torn the body into quarters, throwing the pieces onto the floor and promising revenge on his advisors. It is hard to know what sort of a king Edward would have made had he survived, and without the shaping influences of his childhood, but he was regarded as a somewhat haughty and overly self-confident, if highly intelligent, youth. In the early 1550s his health became ever more a concern as he succumbed to smallpox, measles and a worsening of his latent tuberculosis. He developed a sickly cough, and his bloated, scab-ridden body became repellent to his servants. Dudley (by now Duke of Northumberland) persuaded Edward to disinherit his step-sisters Mary and Elizabeth by recognising his Protestant cousin, and Dudley's daughter-in-law, Lady Jane Grey as his successor. Dudley kept Edward alive, and in great agony, by means of a 'wise woman' and some dubious ointments, just long enough to make appropriate arrangements.

On the afternoon of 6 July 1553 Edward finally relinquished his fragile hold on life, during a great storm that had blown for two days. He was not yet 16 years old. He died in Greenwich Palace, a newly-built royal residence outside London to which he had been removed for better nursing. Little remains of this great Tudor palace except some tiles from the Chapel uncovered, and covered up again, in 2006, and its foundations under the present Grand Square. There are of course many outstanding buildings from the seventeenth century and after, which form the Old Royal Naval College, Trinity College of Music and the University of Greenwich. A stone slab in Grand Square marks the heart of the old Tudor palace (without mentioning Edward VI though).

Mary I, an ardent Catholic, tried to prevent the use of a Protestant ceremony when Edward was finally buried in Westminster Abbey, but eventually gave way, holding instead a Roman Catholic mass at a private chapel for her half-brother. An elegant tomb canopy had been planned but never came about. The basic stone tomb and effigy were destroyed some time in the seventeenth century. All we have today to remember Edward is a memorial flagstone in front of the altar in Henry VII's Lady Chapel in the abbey, marking the spot in which he was buried. It is often hidden by visitors' feet, but does stand out as the only black stone on the beautiful white floor.

LADY JANE GREY

BORN 1537
REIGNED IN 1553 (FOR 9 DAYS)
DIED 12 FEBRUARY 1554
AT: TOWER OF LONDON
BURIED: TOWER OF LONDON

From the sad episode of Edward VI we move on to the tragic case of Lady Jane Grey, queen of England for only nine days, acclaimed when she was but fifteen years old and beheaded at the age of sixteen. Jane was a pretty, highly intelligent and popular girl, granddaughter of Henry VIII's younger sister Mary Tudor and Thomas Brandon, who was the son of Henry VII's standard bearer at the Battle of Bosworth and who had died defending the latter from Richard III's final, desperate attack. Mary and Thomas had a daughter, Frances, who married the lord Henry Grey. Their daughter Lady Jane Grey was therefore of a family much favoured by the Tudor line, and a great niece of Henry VIII.

Throughout Edward VI's short reign, his sister Mary was recognised as the next in line to the throne, assuming Edward did not have any children himself. When Dudley, the Duke of Northumberland and astute controller of Edward's minority, realised that his personal hold on power was about to end, he decided to change the succession. Using Mary's ardent Catholicism to persuade the Protestant Edward that England's new religion was facing certain extinction, Dudley had the dying Edward nominate Lady Jane Grey as his rightful successor. In the meantime Dudley married his son Lord Guilford to Jane, and hoped to rule the country through his influence over the young couple.

Jane protested throughout, both against the marriage and her nomination as queen. She stated clearly, on several occasions, that she had no right and no desire to be queen. As a fifteen year old girl she did of course have little say in the matter, and was proclaimed Queen on 10 July, just four days after Edward's death. Mary fought back, raising a force in Norfolk. People flocked to Mary's cause, most feeling strongly that Mary had the natural right to be their queen. On 19 July Mary was proclaimed Queen and Lady Jane Grey sent to the Tower of London. Here she was kept more as a guest than a prisoner as Mary did not want to punish her innocent and likeable second cousin. Jane's fate was sealed however by a number of rebellions against Mary's proposed marriage to the Catholic Philip of Spain. Mary realised that Jane could be a rallying point for further Protestant rebellions, and reluctantly signed her death warrant.

Poor Jane faced her death with exemplary composure, writing letters of farewell and giving away her possessions. From her window in the Tower she saw her husband Guilford led to the scaffold and then his decapitated body driven back in a cart. A few minutes later she was led to her own scaffold on Tower Green where she seemed to falter at the last, crying out in blindfolded confusion "What shall I do? Where is it?" Her attendants soon led her to the block where the executioner swiftly beheaded her.

There is a beautiful glass memorial to Jane and to others who were beheaded at the Tower. This is in front of the chapel, although one contemporary account states that Jane's execution was in fact on the grassy area next to the White Tower. Jane's small body was buried under a slab in the small chapel of St. Peter ad Vincula in the Tower. The chapel is open late in the day to visitors, and earlier for guided tours.

63. The monument in the Tower of London marking the spot near where Lady Jane Grey was beheaded.

64. The chapel of St. Peter ad Vincula in which Lady Jane Grey is buried. In the foreground is Tower Green and the memorial to those beheaded there.

MARY I 'BLOODY MARY'

♟ BORN 1516

❖ REIGNED FROM 1553 TO 1558

☧ DIED 17 NOVEMBER 1558

AT: ST. JAMES'S PALACE, LONDON

BURIED: WESTMINSTER ABBEY

England's first crowned Queen regnant is mostly remembered today as 'Bloody Mary' for the hundreds of Protestants she had burned, starved and beheaded in a futile attempt at bringing Catholicism back to England. It is a shame that this pretty, determined and principled woman should be recalled so, but it is true that there is little of her reign to be celebrated. Mary had a troubled youth, going from adored, spoiled daughter of Henry VIII and Catherine of Aragon to illegitimate outcast, subjected to her father's indifference or wrath as he saw fit. She found and lost favour again and again as Henry moved through his wives, reaching an uneasy cordiality with her brother Edward VI who barely tolerated her Catholic worship. Never one to give up a fight, something she inherited from her courageous mother, Mary wrested rightful control of the throne from the usurper Lady Jane Grey in July 1553 and almost at once started to pursue her dream of re-integrating England into the Catholic fold.

The subject of faith was to be the central concern for Mary, rather than her womanhood. For centuries England had resisted having a Queen, believing women to be ineffectual rulers who would wreck the country by falling prey to the demands of evil, powerful men. Under Henry VII the key requirement for the monarch had moved away from being a warrior-king to being someone who could govern well with the wise advice of trusted counsellors. The English therefore had less of an issue with Mary as a woman than they did with Mary as a Catholic. Mary showed little flexibility in this. And whereas there were many Catholics who supported her approach, there were many more Protestants equally determined to resist. There were also hundreds of landowners unwilling to give back to the church the former abbeys and church property that they had been given by Henry VIII. Mary's marriage to the very Catholic Philip of Spain further heightened animosity towards her.

It is hard to be sympathetic to Mary from a national point of view. However she is entirely pitiable at a personal level. Her confused upbringing, the treatment she received from her once-loving father and the naïve attitude that her sheltered education engendered, all did little to prepare her for the throne. Mary truly loved her husband Philip, and believed that he had been sent by God to help her divine judgment, but he was completely uninterested in her. She pined for him when he was absent, which was essentially all of their short marriage. She loved children and longed for her own, despite marrying at the age of 38 and nearly at the end of her child-bearing years. Twice she thought she was pregnant, once coming close to her full-term before her swelling began to reduce, revealing itself to be an abdominal infection. She died, at St. James's Palace, probably of cancer of the ovary, an unhappy and unfulfilled woman, with the stain of blood on her memory forever.

The Tudor palace, unlike the great palaces of Whitehall, Greenwich and Richmond, still survives today. Unfortunately it is used as the London residence of the Princess Royal and for State occasions, so is closed to visitors. You can however get a good view of the outside from Marlborough Road and St. James's Street. Mary's heart is still at St. James's Palace. It was removed from her body and buried in a casket beneath the choir stalls in the Chapel Royal at the Palace, itself visible next to the Gatehouse.

Mary's body was buried in a vault in Henry VII's Lady Chapel in Westminster Abbey. Although a monument was planned, none was built. Instead Mary is commemorated by a small amount of script on the magnificent monument to her half-sister Elizabeth I in the north aisle. Overshadowed by Elizabeth in history and overshadowed by her in remembrance.

Right: 65. The Tudor Gatehouse of St. James's Palace from St. James's Street.

Below: 66. Last resting place of Mary's heart, the Chapel Royal at St. James's Palace, London.

Elizabeth I 'Gloriana' and 'The Virgin Queen'

⚱ Born 1533

✠ Reigned from 1558 to 1603

✝ Died 24 March 1603

   At: Richmond Palace, Surrey

   Buried: Westminster Abbey

The very mention of Elizabeth I conjures images of England at its most glorious, a happy land ruled by a strong queen. Although historical sentimentality tends to get in the way of reality, it is true that under Elizabeth England shone as a world power, and that 'the Virgin Queen' really was one of our most powerful and fascinating monarchs.

Elizabeth's strength came from two sources. Firstly, her natural intellect and shrewd political judgment, and secondly her terrifying upbringing. Her birth was a huge disappointment to her father Henry VIII who longed for a son. Her mother Anne Boleyn was beheaded when Elizabeth was three years old. Not only did she have no mother to raise and protect her, but the very sight of Elizabeth was a reminder to Henry of the woman he had once loved to distraction but who was now a very bitter memory. Consequently Henry declared Elizabeth illegitimate, and at best ignored her, though he did provide a comfortable household and an excellent education for her. She had to be careful with her father to avoid his unpredictable and violent behaviour. During her elder half-sister Mary's reign, Elizabeth faced persecution, imprisonment and the threat of execution for her Protestant ways and for being a potential rallying point for dissatisfied, anti-Catholic rebels.

Elizabeth learned through experience how to preserve her life and her position. Her relative seclusion from court life also gave her time to develop her knowledge of Latin, music, horse-riding and other high-born pursuits. It must have been with great relief when Elizabeth acceded to the throne after the death of Mary, safer in the position of ultimate power than she had ever been before.

Elizabeth was a shrewd ruler, using her status as a supposed 'weak and feeble' woman to her full advantage, manipulating her male advisors and using marriage as a bargaining counter. She could be stately, majestic and ferocious yet never lost her love of dancing and her capricious, girlish ways. She took the art of power dressing to supreme heights, overawing visitors with jewels, dazzling costumes and make-up. The people and events of her long reign are legendary – the defeat of the Armada, Drake, the many suitors, Raleigh, the Virginia colony named after her, Shakespeare, Mary, Queen of Scots, to name but a few. Elizabeth retained her faculties almost to the end, when she caught a midwinter cold. She retired to her palace in Richmond and soon succumbed to a form of pneumonia accompanied by a great melancholy. Although so little remains of the once-beautiful palace it is easy to imagine Elizabeth riding on her horse through the surviving stone and brick arch opposite the green.

Her monument in Westminster Abbey is magnificent, although many visitors are confused by the fact that the inscriptions are for both her and her predecessor Mary I. It is odd that two women so antagonistic in life should be buried together. Despite the inscription (translated) 'Consorts both in throne and grave, here rest we two sisters, Elizabeth and Mary, in the hope of one Resurrection' it is Elizabeth's tomb that is on top of her sister's, and only Elizabeth's effigy that is visible. The face is a verisimilitude having been taken from a death-mask.

67. The main gateway to Richmond Palace and one of the few surviving Tudor buildings. The arms above the arch are Henry VII's, and the blue plaque states 'Richmond Palace, a residence of King Henry VII, King Henry VIII, Queen Elizabeth I'.

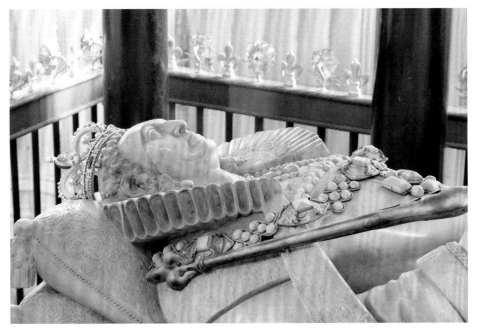

68. Elizabeth's effigy above her tomb in Westminster Abbey.

JAMES I

- BORN 1566
- REIGNED FROM 1603 TO 1625
- DIED 27 MARCH 1625
  AT: THEOBALDS, HERTFORDSHIRE
  BURIED: WESTMINSTER ABBEY

Coarse, cowardly, dirty, openly homosexual (in a time when it caused genuine outrage) and garrulous beyond patience, James I was as unmajestic a figure as ever there was. Strange to find then that he was an ardent believer in the divine right of kings, that kings were appointed by God to rule over their subjects, and that to question a king's authority was an act of blasphemy. His subjects may well have questioned what right such a disgusting and fractious man had to rule over them in such a high-handed fashion.

James had been King of Scotland since he was fourteen months old, and on that throne for thirty-six years when he learned that the dying Elizabeth had named him heir to the English throne. James was son of Mary, Queen of Scots, and descended from Margaret Tudor, Henry VIII's sister, who had married James IV of Scotland. His mother had been forced to abdicate in the face of public horror over her involvement in the murder of her despised husband Henry Stuart, Lord Darnley – from whom the Stuart dynasty took their name. James was brought up in an atmosphere of terror, including the murder of at least two of his regents, and under a strict religious and intellectual education. It isn't surprising that, with his fearful nature and his weak spindly body, he took to wearing padded quilt jackets to protect himself from assassins' knives.

Despite the antagonism between the Scots and the English, James was in fact welcomed joyously as he travelled down from Edinburgh to London in 1603. And James welcomed the

69. Theobalds Park, Georgian descendant of the former Tudor palace.

wealthy, stable English throne with glee after years of relative poverty and insecurity. It didn't take long for them fall out though, as James' arrogance, the roughness of his courtiers and his tactless criticism of English military failings began to grate. His passions were hunting, reading and talking, all of which he indulged in frequently. James' sharp intellect, Protestant upbringing and love of books led him to oversee personally the publication of the authoritative King James Bible, whose influence since has been immense. The Gunpowder Plot is about the only other truly memorable event in this monarch's reign.

Towards the end of his reign, James suffered from an ulcerated face, incessant drooling from his overly large tongue and was in constant need of physical support, usually from a favoured young man. Always in pain, he retired to his favourite palace of Theobalds, near Cheshunt in Hertfordshire, where his lover the Earl of Buckingham is alleged to have hastened his inevitable demise with doses of arsenic. Theobalds was never a great palace such as Whitehall or Greenwich, but was rather an impressive Tudor manor house with considerable royal additions. Unfortunately it deteriorated in the early eighteenth century and was replaced with a grand, brick, Georgian pile. Today it is well looked after as a hotel/conference centre, in pleasant grounds, and well worth a look, though there is little to honour the memory of its former royal resident.

James was buried under Henry VII's monument in the Lady Chapel in Westminster Abbey. He was, oddly, much mourned, with thousands turning up to his lying in state and his funeral, providing a neat symmetry to his reign. No monument was built, establishing an unwonted precedent, for not one of the Stuart dynasty has a monument on their grave in England. Instead James has a stone slab with his name inscribed, just behind Henry VII's monument and very near Oliver Cromwell's memorial stone.

CHARLES I 'THE MARTYR'

⚱ BORN 1600
✠ REIGNED FROM 1625 TO 1649
✝ DIED 30 JANUARY 1649
AT: WHITEHALL, LONDON
BURIED: ST. GEORGE'S CHAPEL, WINDSOR

It is hard not to feel sorry for Charles I, but it is also hard not to view him with a degree of contempt. A man who was not supposed to be king famously became the only English king to be beheaded, a martyr for a cause that really needed no martyr. Whilst Charles was by no means one of England's worst monarchs, his insufferable arrogance and belief in his divine right to rule led to a violent schism between the crown and Parliament that could have been resolved more peaceably over time. But did his 'martyrdom' benefit England (or rather Great Britain by now) in the long term? Perhaps this sudden and relatively early resolution of some of the conflicts between the new and old seats of power acted as a safety valve, letting off a good deal of the pressure which blew up so much more spectacularly in other countries, such as France and Russia, in later centuries. The Civil War was a tragic and unnecessary event in our history but was also the catalyst for a good deal of change from which we benefit even today.

As a child Charles was a sickly, weak boy and was not expected to live. He was the exact opposite of his older brother Henry, who was admired as an intelligent, energetic, affable, majestic youth, destined to make a fine Henry IX. Charles was excruciatingly shy, caused partly no doubt by his severe stammer, and by having to live with such an extrovert and often coarse family. He was studious and intelligent but not brilliant, and was taught in a somewhat severe Protestant environment. His later passion for sensuous, Italianate art was at odds with his religious upbringing, indeed his marriage to the Catholic daughter of the French King brought accusations of popery, which Charles was swift to deny.

Charles tried to rule alone, without Parliament's advice, as a divinely appointed king should. He wasn't really up to the job as he shared his father's ineptitude with money, brought in taxes that were unpopular with landowners and tried to enforce a form of Protestantism that caused rifts in England and outright war in Scotland. By 1642 flags had been raised for King and for Parliament, and the Civil War started. Despite a number of indecisive early battles, the Parliamentarian forces, superbly led by Oliver Cromwell and his New Model Army eventually gained the upper hand. Charles refused to accept a new constitution in which he would have been King with limited powers, and was eventually brought to trial and executed by a Parliament now desperate to rule as a republic.

Charles's bearing at both his trial and execution are legendary. Refusing to recognise the legitimacy of the court, yet arguing deftly against his accusers, he was, in the end, forcibly condemned. On a bitterly cold January day, wearing two shirts to prevent a shiver that might be mistaken for cowardice, Charles was led to a scaffold through the first floor window of the Banqueting House of Whitehall Palace where he was beheaded. The Banqueting House is a marvel, and is the only surviving structure from the once massive palace. At the front of the building on Whitehall, on the north side, there is a bust and plaque marking the window through which he was led.

A burial in Westminster Abbey was thought too dangerous, politically, so Charles was buried instead in the more discrete St. George's Chapel, Windsor, in the space reserved for Catherine Parr in Henry VIII's vault. Charles II was unable to raise sufficient funds for a monument, so none was built. In 1837 a marble slab was laid as a memorial to both Charles I and Henry VIII, with brass lettering. You can find this easily near the centre of the quire, just to the west of the memorial slab to George III.

The memorial tablet reads:

HIS MAJESTY KING CHARLES ·I·
PASSED THROUGH THIS HALL AND
OUT OF A WINDOW NEARLY OVER
THIS TABLET TO THE SCAFFOLD
IN WHITEHALL WHERE HE WAS
BEHEADED ON 30ᵗʰ JANUARY 1649

70. Near this memorial lay the scaffold where Charles I was beheaded.

71. The quire of St. George's Chapel. The memorial to Charles I is just visible in the centre of the floor, under the magnificent fan vaulting.

Oliver Cromwell 'The Lord Protector'

- Born 1599
- Ruled from 1653 to 1658
- Died 3 September 1658
  At: Whitehall Palace
  Buried: Westminster Abbey, then Tyburn, London and Sidney Sussex College, Cambridge

Oliver Cromwell was never officially proclaimed King, although he was offered the throne by Parliament. He refused it, after much soul-searching, but instead accepted the title of Lord Protector of the Commonwealth for life and settled into a role that was as good as kingship, barring the crown itself. Many people in England today view Cromwell with, at best, suspicion – for his strict Puritan beliefs, his regicide, the slaughter of garrisons in Drogheda and Wexford in Ireland, his assumption of a hereditary leadership, or maybe just that he represented a class of people who dared to stand up for their beliefs and overthrow autocracy. The extent to which he went to enforce his ideals doesn't always sit well with the English mentality – bloody revolution happens overseas but surely not in England?

His reputation is an injustice to Cromwell, who in many ways was a man much more remarkable and praiseworthy than the kings who preceded and succeeded his Protectorship. He was born into the Huntingdonshire gentry, spending a year at Sidney Sussex College, Cambridge (where he excelled at sports, not at his lessons) before retiring to marriage and life as a farmer. At some point he experienced a religious epiphany, and became convinced that he would serve his country through Puritansim, a strict form of Protestantism that rejected all taints of Catholicism and embraced simplified worship. It was through his advocacy of Puritansim that he became noted as a man of energy and intelligence, and was elected as an MP first for Huntingdon, then Cambridge.

Cromwell's rise to power was remarkable – from leading a troop of 200 lightly armed soldiers in Cambridgeshire at the start of the Civil War in 1642, to foremost general in the Parliamentarian army and proponent of the New Model Army, to uncontested Lord Protector in 1653. He was ruthless and in many respects just an alternative dictator, yet many foreign diplomats admired his dignity and judgment. Despite his strict religious beliefs he aspired to tolerance, bringing back the Jews who had been expelled by Edward I in the thirteenth century, and campaigned for conciliation between sects. His firm rule meant that England was able to experiment with a radical form of government, quasi-military rule and unheard-of levels of taxation without descending into the anarchy that would blight so many other countries.

Cromwell died in Whitehall Palace in 1658 of complications from malaria, a kidney stone and bereavement over the death of his favourite daughter Bessie a month previously. The night of his death witnessed the most severe storm in living memory, with the superstitious claiming it was Satan himself rushing to claim Cromwell's soul.

His body was originally buried in Westminster Abbey, alongside many other prominent Parliamentarians and members of the Cromwell family. With the Restoration of the monarchy in 1660 and the Bill of Attainder, Cromwell's body was exhumed and given the traitor's punishment of hanging at Tyburn, followed by his head being put on a spike outside Westminster Hall for public display. His body is believed to have been thrown into a common gallows pit at Tyburn, though there are numerous alternative and improbable claimants to his grave around the country. Tyburn was a key London gallows for many years before being swallowed up by housing developments. The memorial to the famous 'Tyburn Tree' is almost impossible to get to, stuck as it is on a traffic island at the bottom of Edgware Road, overlooked by Marble Arch and within throwing distance of Speakers Corner.

72. The Banqueting House, sole significant remnant of Whitehall Palace.

73. Near this spot is the pit where Cromwell's body was buried.

74. The Chapel of Sidney Sussex College, Cambridge.

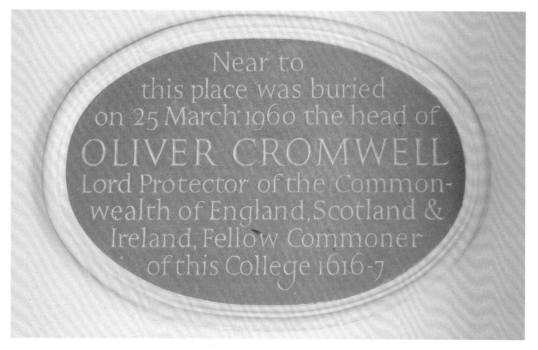

75. The plaque in the entrance hall of the Chapel of Sidney Sussex College, Cambridge, where Cromwell's head is buried in a secret location.

The fate of Cromwell's head is much better documented. It was blown off its spike in a gale during the reign of James II, picked up by a palace guard, then sold and exhibited by a number of entrepreneurs. It was eventually offered to Cromwell's former college at Cambridge where its precise location is kept secret, but is honoured with a plaque near the entrance to the chapel. It is easily found to the right of the Porter's Lodge (where visitors should first check for access.)

In Westminster Abbey there is a small stone in the floor behind Henry VII's tomb, at the entrance to the Royal Air Force Memorial Chapel, marking the former burial place of Oliver Cromwell.

76. Cromwell Avenue, Cheshunt. Richard Cromwell died near here in 1712.

RICHARD CROMWELL 'TUMBLEDOWN DICK' AND 'QUEEN DICK'

    BORN 1626

✱   RULED FROM SEPTEMBER 1658 TO MAY 1659

✞   DIED 12 JULY 1712

       AT: PENGELLY HOUSE, CHESHUNT

       BURIED: HURSLEY, HAMPSHIRE

Under the constitution adopted in 1657 as the 'Humble Petition and Advice', Oliver Cromwell was allowed to nominate his successor. Although this seemed to hark back to the bad old days of the monarchy, a smooth succession of power was in everybody's interests. At this time Richard Cromwell was Oliver's third and eldest surviving son, but had shown little interest in statesmanship earlier in life. He was happy living on his wife Dorothy's estate in Hampshire, engaging in field sports, neglecting religion and acting as a Justice of the Peace. From the 1650s and the establishment of the Protectorate, he began to accompany his father on important occasions and sat as MP for Cambridge University, so that in 1658 he was ready to be proclaimed Lord Protector upon Oliver's death.

Richard was a smart, tactful man but not as commanding and forceful as his father. Nor was he as ambitious. His real problem however lay with his lack of soldiering expertise. Oliver had won huge respect from the powerful army for his leadership qualities in the Civil War, but Richard was derided as 'Tumbledown Dick' or 'Prince Richard' by generals who refused to hand overall command to an untried 'gentleman'. Despite several clever political manoeuvres Richard was repeatedly denied access to funds and was eventually forced to renounce his Protectorship, just before Charles II returned. He fled the country, in debt and in fear for his life, living in France away from his family for the next 20 years.

From his return to England in 1680 to his death in 1712 at the grand old age of 85, Richard Cromwell lived mostly with Baron Pengelly in Cheshunt, under the assumed name of John Clarke. The original seventeenth-century house burned down in 1888 and was replaced with cottages near the building now called Pengelly House. Nothing can be seen of the original, and the only memorial to Cromwell is a nearby street in his name.

A few records point to Richard dying at Hursley House in Hampshire, where he was lord of the manor through his wife. Richard's son Oliver (the second) had died there in 1705 and it is thought that Richard may have returned to live there after that date. The current building is a later development and of rather sombre build. It is an IBM headquarters.

Richard was buried in the very pleasant All Saints' Church, Hursley, but nobody knows exactly where his bones lie, or indeed where the vault is. The famous Victorian minister and one time vicar of All Saints, John Keble, hated all things to do with Puritanism so removed any mention of the Cromwell family when he rebuilt the church in 1848.

The Cromwell family memorial, in grey marble, was later re-erected in the tower, on your right as you enter from the north porch. In 1993 a plaque was put up next to the memorial to commemorate the village's famous connection.

77. All Saints' Church, Hursley, last resting place of Richard Cromwell.

78. The Cromwell family memorial that lists Richard Cromwell, and the 1993 commemorative plaque to the left.

CHARLES II 'THE MERRY MONARCH' AND 'OLD ROWLEY'

⚱ BORN 1630
✠ REIGNED FROM 1660 TO 1685
✝ DIED 6 FEBRUARY 1685
   AT: WHITEHALL PALACE
   BURIED: WESTMINSTER ABBEY

Six foot two inches tall, swarthy and with luxuriant black curly hair, Charles II was famously attractive to women. He recognised at least a dozen bastards from consorts such as Nell Gwynne and Barbara Villiers, and probably had more through dozens of mistresses and paid courtesans. His court was renowned for its debauchery, not only a reflection of its master's lusty, pleasure-seeking nature but also a reaction against the stern and grey rule of the Commonwealth. Yet Charles was much more than this. He was a much-loved monarch, a sponsor of the sciences, an affable and equitable man who found time for everyone, and put everyone at their comfort in his presence. He was a straight-talking man of easy compromise with Parliament and with those who had ushered in Republicanism. Some may put it down to laziness, but Charles was a shrewd, worldly man who had suffered much in his youth, and knew exactly what it took to re-establish the Stuart line on the throne.

From the age of 12, when he joined his father Charles I at the Battle of Edgehill in the first Civil War, to the age of 30 when he was welcomed back rapturously as King, Charles led a nomadic and often penniless existence. Proclamation as King of Scotland in 1651 was followed by a failed invasion of England and weeks of adventures dressed as a labourer, with narrow escapes from soldiers (including the probably mythical sojourn in an oak tree, after which hundreds of Royal Oak pubs take their name). Nine years of poverty, wandering around France and Flanders, seeking refuge in sexual excess and despairing of ever taking back his inheritance aged Charles somewhat. But it also taught him a lot, in terms of practicalities, getting on with people and the value of humour in confronting problems. When, in 1660, Charles returned to a wildly celebrating London, he re-ignited a love of life that we see today in the works of Pepys and Evelyn, the diarists, and the Restoration dramatists. The Royal Society thrived under his approval, fostering giants such as Sir Christopher Wren and Sir Isaac Newton.

The capture of New Amsterdam, renamed New York, happened during Charles' reign, as did the Great Plague, and the Great Fire of London in 1666. Charles was in the midst of the flames, throwing buckets of water into the firestorm to try to save his capital, sweating and choking alongside the poor residents of the city. Despite his general appeal to commoners and nobles alike, Charles did have his detractors, notably those who criticised the louche behaviour of his court, and those who feared he might bring Catholicism back to England. Indeed, Charles did become a Catholic, but only on his deathbed where he took his first and last communion from an old priest whom he had met after the Battle of Worcester in 1651. It is ironic that the prolific child-maker Charles had no children from his loving marriage to Catherine of Braganza; one of his legacies was therefore to plunge Britain back into a religious crisis as the throne passed to his Catholic brother James.

Charles died rather unexpectedly at the age of 55, of chronic kidney failure, hastened by several doctors administering over fifty hack medicines and treatments, including burning his skin with hot irons. Charles was characteristically good-natured throughout. Just before he died, Charles requested that the curtains in his chamber at Whitehall Palace be opened so he could see dawn over the River Thames one last time. Charles was buried in a vault in the south aisle of Henry VII's Lady Chapel at Westminster Abbey. Like his father and grandfather, there is no monument, just a simple stone slab in the floor in front of the altar.

79. The inscribed stone above Charles II's vault in Westminster Abbey.

80. The inner courtyard of the chateau of St-Germain-en-Laye on the outskirts of Paris.

JAMES II

- ♤ BORN 1633
- ✠ REIGNED FROM 1685 TO 1688
- ✟ DIED 16 SEPTEMBER 1701
  AT: ST-GERMAIN-EN-LAYE, YVELINES, FRANCE
  BURIED: ST-GERMAIN-EN-LAYE, YVELINES, FRANCE AND NUMEROUS OTHERS

James II suffered in comparison to the highly popular Charles II. Like his brother he was tall, handsome (by most accounts even more handsome) and sexually voracious. Unlike his brother, he was serious to the point of being dour, aloof and politically unaware. He was undoubtedly a brave man, rising to the rank of Lieutenant-General in the French Army by the age of 21, distinguishing himself in several battles whilst in exile from Oliver Cromwell's government. Even then his supporters noted that his high intelligence was not matched by his astuteness, and that although he was expert at managing details he was unable to see the bigger picture.

James's conversion to Catholicism during Charles' reign caused a longstanding crisis over the succession, and reignited fears about papist plots to overthrow English Protestantism. Charles was unable to produce a legitimate child, so James was heir to the throne. James's daughters, and next in line to the throne, Mary and Anne, were being raised as Protestants so at first people were not too anxious about the long-term Catholic threat. A series of events, including the Titus Oates affair, and the surprising birth of a healthy son and new heir by James's Catholic wife Mary of Modena, turned the situation. Many sought to implicate James in Catholic plots, and started a rumour that his son was not his own but had instead been smuggled into the birthing chamber in a warming-pan. James was in fact very loyal to his brother, and the warming-plan plot baseless, but the country was uneasy.

At his accession, James promised not to impose his religion on the nation, and got off to a good start with Parliament. Circumstances deteriorated however as James sought to move Catholic friends into important positions, despite the recent Test Act discouraging such appointments, and continental Europe surged towards religious conflict. James also started to suffer physically and mentally, probably due to a syphilitic infection, becoming less tolerant and more fixated on his religion. In 1688 a group of magnates invited the Protestant William of Orange, husband of James' daughter Mary, to invade England. James fled rather than fight, and what came to be termed 'The Glorious Revolution' bloodlessly ushered in England's first and only joint monarchy.

During his exile James made one attempt to regain his crown, but his Irish and French army was defeated by William at the Battle of the Boyne. James retired to the protection of Louis XIV in France, where he found solace in hunting, raising his son James Stuart, later known as the Old Pretender, and daughter Louisa, and reminiscing. He died at the Chateau of St-Germain-en-Laye, lent to him by a France which found such a potential thorn in the side of the old enemy England too tempting to ignore. The chateau is open to the public as the National Museum of Archaeology. It is a fine building and a fine museum, but the number of former royal rooms you can visit is limited.

James's body was scattered to various parts of France, but today doesn't really seem to be buried anywhere. His body was laid in state in the Chapel of St. Edmund in the Convent of the English Benedictines in Rue Saint-Jacques, Paris, awaiting transferral to Westminster Abbey. This never happened. During the French Revolution his coffin was broken open and the contents probably thrown into a common burial pit nearby. They have certainly been lost. The convent itself was mostly destroyed, and is now a school of the performing arts at no. 269, near the beautiful Val du Grâce.

His brain was put in a casket in an obelisk in the chapel at the Scots' College in Paris, and his heart buried at the Convent of the Visitandine Nuns on the Trocadéro, also in Paris. Whereas the Convent has now completely disappeared beneath the Palais de Chaillot, the former College can be seen at 65 Rue du Cardinal Lemoine. There is even a Paris History panel outside referring to the brain inside, but the building is now used by nuns and is not generally open to the public.

His other organs were buried at the English Church in St. Omer (formerly the Church of the English Jesuit College, and now part of a school) and in the parish church of St-Germain-en-Laye, opposite the chateau. Fortunately the casket containing some of his organs in St-Germain-en-Laye was found in the nineteenth century. Queen Victoria erected a monument to him in that church so we at least have a more appropriate memorial to our last Catholic king. There are also two plaques on the outside wall, one Victoria's and one from the Franco-Scottish Association. Inside is the more grandiose monument, alluding to James's finer qualities.

81. 269 Rue Saint-Jacques in Paris, in the centre of the photo. James's bones are likely to be buried near here, but it is uncertain. The dome of the Val du Grâce can just be seen in the background.

Histoire de Paris
Collège des Ecossais

L'immeuble sur rue a été construit de 1662 à 1665 par Robert Barclay qui dirige le collège et le séminaire des Ecossais. Achevée en 1672, la chapelle possède un mausolée où repose dans une urne en bronze doré, le cerveau de Jacques II d'Angleterre, mort à Saint-Germain-en-Laye en 1701. Transformé en prison sous la Terreur, le collège fut rendu à l'église anglaise en 1806, et loué par un établissement d'enseignement

de 1815 à 1914. A la suite de la rectification de la pente de la rue en 1685, le rez-de-chaussée de la façade sur rue devint premier étage. Mais la façade sur jardin est restée intacte.

82. The panel outside the old Scots' College in Paris.

83. The monument to James II in the parish church of St-Germain-en-Laye.

84. The former English Church of St. Omer, in the Pas de Calais.

85. Kensington Palace viewed from the sunken garden in spring.

MARY II

☈ BORN 1662

✚ REIGNED FROM 1689 TO 1694 (JOINTLY)

✝ DIED 28 DECEMBER 1694

AT: KENSINGTON PALACE, LONDON

BURIED: WESTMINSTER ABBEY

Mary II was the eldest daughter of James II by his first wife, the relatively low-born Anne Hyde. Because of her father's Catholic leanings, Mary was brought up as a Protestant at the insistence of the then king, Charles II. The country's stability depended on there being as little Catholic threat as possible to the succession, and Mary was, in the absence to date of any male children, next in line to the throne. Her position stayed as such all the way through Charles's reign and then her father's, right up to just before the deposition of James, when his wife miraculously bore him a healthy son. By then it was too late. England refused any longer to countenance a Catholic king and invited the Protestant William of Orange and his wife Mary to succeed, annulling any right that James' son would normally have had to the throne.

As a child Mary was a lively, friendly girl, not overly endowed with intelligence but keen to please and to be liked. Her mother died when Mary was nine, and she was brought up outside her father's influence, so she relied on others for mother and father figures. In later life she was the perfect counter-balance to her taciturn and grim husband, always ready to talk to visitors and handle court affairs with grace and charm. Despite her easy-going nature, Mary was unable to keep a good relationship with her nearest family. She fell out with her younger sister Anne over the latter's friendship with the Churchills, barely speaking to her in her final years, and after 1688 didn't even try to reconcile herself to her father, whose crown she had effectively usurped.

Mary's marriage to William was in the end a happy one though it started off badly. Mary was tall, beautiful and only fifteen when she was told she had to marry the short, slightly-hunchbacked and dour William. She cried throughout her wedding and for days after, but in a while came to appreciate her husband and his Dutch court, treating William with affection despite his many infidelities and cold manner. He completely dominated her both emotionally and politically, but she seems to have been happy to go along with this, her biggest disappointment being unable to produce any children.

She holds a unique position in reigning jointly with her husband. Indeed the law had to be changed so much to accommodate joint monarchs that the couple could not be officially appointed, and then crowned, until 1689, several months after James had fled. In her short reign as queen, Mary endeared herself to her ministers as hard-working and open, in complete contrast to the wretched William whose popularity went from bad to worse. When, in 1694, at the early age of 32, she contracted smallpox and died, Mary was genuinely mourned by the nation, and given a massive funeral. William himself was devastated, and continued to rule alone for another eight years.

One of Mary's greatest contributions to the country was the construction of Kensington Palace. Built in what was then a country village as a retreat from London for the asthmatic William, it is a small and beautiful palace that is now open to the public. Mary died in her bedchamber in the side of the palace that is called the Queen's apartments, and which has a notably homely, Dutch influence.

Despite her lavish funeral at Westminster Abbey, there is no monument to Mary, nor is there one to William. Her name is inscribed on a flagstone before the altar in the south aisle of the Lady Chapel in Westminster Abbey, above or near her vault, but that is all we have to remind us of her final resting place. It is very easy to miss, overshadowed as it is by the magnificent tomb of Mary Queen of Scots.

WILLIAM III

- ☖ BORN 1650
- ✠ REIGNED FROM 1689 (JOINTLY) TO 1694 AND 1694 TO 1702 (SOLELY)
- ♱ DIED 8 MARCH 1702
  AT: KENSINGTON PALACE, LONDON
  BURIED: WESTMINSTER ABBEY

As a Protestant and member of the ruling family that had united Holland (or the United Provinces as it then was) and successfully fought off its much bigger and Catholic neighbour France, William was a hero to many northern Europeans. He was also a fabulously wealthy hero, with an annual income greater than Charles II's. It was not surprising then that influential Englishmen should look to William as a saviour from the Catholic threat, especially as he had a moderate claim to the English throne, through being the grandson of Charles I by the latter's daughter Mary. He was also married to the first in line to the throne, another Mary.

Although the crown was officially offered to Mary, it was William who had been invited to invade England to get rid of James II, and his pride refused to allow him to play second fiddle to his wife. Parliament therefore offered a joint monarchy, quite unprecedented in English history, and requiring special laws to be passed, followed by a further Act of Parliament to determine the succession. It is a reflection of the flexibility of English government that this could happen, and of their passionate desire to defend Protestantism at all costs. It was by no means an easy thing to persuade William to leave his beloved, and threatened, Holland. And Parliament knew they would face decades of pressure from James and his descendants who had the moral right to the throne, despite James' 'abdication by default' (he fled the country rather than face William's forces.)

William was not an impressive figure. Short, with prominent features and a mild hunchback, he was a silent, gloomy type who never much liked the frivolity of his new English subjects, preferring his Dutch court. He was asthmatic, suffering terribly in stuffy rooms and from London's polluted atmosphere. He also seems to have been sexually ambiguous, being suspected of homosexual relationships with a number of favourites as well as having affairs with numerous court ladies. Many of his years as king were spent overseas in war with France, and he had little time for English governance. During his reign there were attempts to suppress the Catholics of Highland Scotland, leading to the Massacre of Glencoe, and England joined the War of the Spanish Succession to try to prevent French control of the vast Habsburg empire.

William met his end whilst riding to Hampton Court. His horse stepped on a molehill, throwing its rider. William suffered a broken collar bone, which became infected, and he caught pneumonia on his return to Kensington Palace. He died there in his bedchamber in the King's apartments, mourned by few if any in England. Whilst he was a cold and unattractive man, it is touching to note that a locket of Mary's hair and her wedding ring were discovered in a pouch hanging next to his heart. This unique partnership was much more than just a shared throne.

He was buried without pomp in the same vault as Mary in Westminster Abbey. There is no memorial to him, as with Mary, just a simple slab with his name inscribed in front of the altar in the south aisle of the Lady Chapel.

WILLIAM III
OF ORANGE
KING OF GREAT BRITAIN
AND IRELAND 1689-1702
PRESENTED BY WILLIAM II
GERMAN EMPEROR AND
KING OF PRUSSIA TO
KING EDWARD VII FOR
THE BRITISH NATION
1907

86. The statue of William III at the front of Kensington Palace, the house that he and Mary built as their main London residence.

ANNE

⚀ BORN 1665

✠ REIGNED FROM 1702 TO 1714

✠ DIED 1 AUGUST 1714

AT: KENSINGTON PALACE, LONDON

BURIED: WESTMINSTER ABBEY

During the reign of Queen Anne, Great Britain started becoming truly 'great'. For so many centuries on the fringe of European events, the country established itself as a power to be reckoned with, and started to develop the form of government that we see today. The 1707 Act of Union formally joined England with Scotland under one parliament. Parliament itself began to divide into parties, Whigs and Tories, representing different views on political control. John Churchill, Duke of Marlborough, built a formidable army that conquered the mighty French at the battles of Blenheim, Ramillies, Oudenaarde and Malplaquet, adding land forces to the already renowned naval forces at the country's disposal. Great men flourished in all walks of life, such as Kneller, Wren, Swift, Pope and Walpole. And Britain took on an air of refinement and elegance that is encapsulated in the Queen Anne style of architecture and furniture so highly regarded today.

What of Anne herself? Some argue that Anne had nothing to do with these developments, that she was merely a dull figurehead who was neither capable of understanding nor interested in following the great events of her times. Others argue that Anne's uncontentious yet conscientious attitude to monarchy helped empower her subjects to achieve what they did, whereas previous kings had too much self-interest and power to let the country truly prosper. There are elements of truth in both. Dim and slightly ridiculous she may have been, but Anne is praiseworthy.

Anne is also a pitiable character. She suffered from agonising bouts of joint inflammation or gout. She was plain and very short-sighted, with a terrible squint. She had eighteen pregnancies, thirteen of which were stillbirths or miscarriages, four of whom died in infancy. The only surviving child was a delicate boy who died suddenly at the age of eleven. Anne took to overeating and drinking, her naturally plump form becoming so obese that she had to be carried to her coronation and lifted around her palaces with ropes and pulleys. She was also shy and desperately in need of intimates, most famously the overbearing Sarah Churchill who caused much friction between Anne and her close family.

Anne bore her illnesses and personal tragedies with much dignity, for which she must be admired. Her eventual death at the age of 49 at her beloved Kensington Palace was probably a blessing, putting an end to so much pain. As she had no surviving children, Anne was the last of the Stuart line. Like all the Stuarts, she has no monument in Westminster Abbey, where she was buried in a massive square coffin to accommodate her vast bulk. She too is commemorated by a simple inscription on a flagstone in front of the altar in the south aisle of the Lady Chapel.

GEORGE I

      BORN 1660
      REIGNED FROM 1714 TO 1727
      DIED 11 JUNE 1727
      AT: OSNABRÜCK CASTLE, GERMANY
      BURIED: LEINESCHLOSS, HANOVER, GERMANY THEN HERRENHÄUSEN
      GARDENS, HANOVER

Of all the monarchs, George I seems the least appealing. He was certainly unpopular with his subjects of the day, although many were happy enough there was a Protestant king on the throne rather than a Catholic. His accession came via the 1701 Act of Settlement which proclaimed Sophia of Hanover, grand-daughter of James I, the designated heir. Sophia died just two months before Anne, so her son George, already Elector of Hanover and of the Holy Roman Empire, was next in line.

George made no attempt to learn English, nor to hide the fact that he would much rather be in Hanover. He surrounded himself with German courtiers and brought his simple, uncultured taste to his London court. Some twenty years previously George had murdered his wife's lover and locked the pretty Sophia Dorothea in a castle, where she was to remain for the rest of her life. In the meantime he took on several mistresses, involving them in court and national descisions. His two favourites were nicknamed 'The Elephant' and 'The Maypole', being respectively squat and fat, and tall and skinny. His son hated him for locking up his mother and the hatred was returned with passion, only the tactful intervention of Robert Walpole tempering the situation to a state of icy hostility. George's indifference to governance led to corruption and escalating party politics, though this had a benefit in shifting power further away from the monarch towards Parliament. Thousands of people lost money, and many committed suicide, over the 'South Sea Bubble' fiasco. Whilst not directly caused by the king, people blamed him because of the financial impropriety emanating from his court.

One positive from his reign is that Handel was brought from Germany to London, where he composed music especially for George's boat trips along the Thames. Other than that, and a secured succession, the cold, dull king with impressive double standards brought little to the nation. It was on one of several trips home to Hanover that he fell ill from a stroke near the Dutch/German border. He proceeded to Osnabrück Castle where he died, in the same room in which he had been born 67 years earlier. The castle was originally home to the Prince-Bishop of Osnabrück but is now offices for the town's university. It remains an impressive building despite the ravages of Allied bombing in the second world war.

Although moves were made to bring his body back to England, it was eventually decided that he should be buried in his homeland. George was laid to rest in the chapel of the Leineschloss, a castle complex in the city of Hanover. The much rebuilt Leineschloss is now home to the Diet, or Parliament, of Lower Saxony.

The castle complex was so badly damaged during the second world war that his tomb was moved to the royal Hanoverian mausoleum in the Berggarten area of the Herrenhäusen Gardens. Inside the mausoleum are the remains of six Hanoverian kings and queens from 1679 to 1841. It is unfortunately no longer open to the public, but the Herrenhäusen Gardens are, and are amongst the largest and most beautiful in Europe.

87. Osnabrück Castle.

88. Leineschloss, Hanover. The river Leine runs to the back of the building. Inside are photos of the area in the aftermath of bombing.

89. George I's mausoleum in the Herrenhäusen Gardens, Hanover

George II

  ⌂ Born 1683

  ✠ Reigned from 1727 to 1760

  ♱ Died 25 October 1760

     At: Kensington Palace, London

     Buried: Westminster Abbey

The last British king to have been born abroad, and the last king to lead his troops into battle, George II was a prickly character though ultimately a successful ruler. During his reign Britain captured Canada from the French, established influence in India, strangled French dominance in Europe and became the pre-eminent trading hub of the world. The Catholic Jacobite threat was stubbed out once and for all, after the 1745 rising of Bonnie Prince Charlie, and Parliament continued to draw power away from the monarchy under highly capable ministers such as Walpole and Pitt.

George's personal popularity followed a U-shaped curve through his life. As Prince of Wales he had been a model of courtesy and the centre of a sparkling, rival court to his hated father, George I. Young aristocrats and great men from the arts and sciences flocked to his banner. His wife, Caroline of Ansbach, was a pretty, intelligent woman who enjoyed the company of and encouraged genius. Yet as George acceded to the throne, he turned short-tempered, critical and blunt. Never the smartest of men, he was comfortable only when talking about military matters or when barking insults at his courtiers. He grew frustrated with Parliament, sensing that power was being taken away from him yet unable to do anything about it. He spent much time in Hanover and with various mistresses. Like his father had done with him, George hated Frederick, his first-born son. Both he and Caroline openly stated that they wished him dead and out of the line of succession. His popularity in Britain reached a low ebb, possibly even lower than his father's.

Then in 1743 George led his forces to victory over the French at the Battle of Dettingen, in the War of the Austrian Succession. He demonstrated supreme courage and leadership, and returned to London a hero. Despite being 60 years old, and still gruff, he enjoyed a renaissance that saw him through to the end of his reign some 17 years later. He was able to maintain a good relationship with his Prime Minister, William Pitt, and earned the latter's grudging respect. Frederick died, after an accident at a game of cricket, and George was relieved that the throne would pass to his grandson, also George. Ultimately his popularity was achieved almost entirely through the deeds of other men but he was judged by this, and was sincerely mourned at his death.

George died of an aortic aneurism while on his toilet at Kensington Palace. It was a sudden end, and, despite his grand old age of 77 years, quite unexpected. The privy where he died is in the vicinity of the Mantua room, open to visitors to Kensington Palace. He was buried in Westminster Abbey, in the same coffin as his beloved Caroline. Like his immediate forbears he was not given a monument, and only has his name inscribed on a flagstone near the altar in Henry VII's Lady Chapel. It is difficult to find, often obscured by visitors' feet and in fading black letters on a white stone in the floor. He added one more 'last' to his name – the last king to be buried in the Abbey.

90. Westminster Abbey from the west side, burial place of George II. He was the last to follow the tradition established by the first king to be buried there, Henry III.

GEORGE III 'FARMER GEORGE' AND 'MAD KING GEORGE'

🜄 BORN 1738

✠ REIGNED FROM 1760 TO 1820

✟ DIED 29 JANUARY 1820

AT: WINDSOR CASTLE

BURIED: ST. GEORGE'S CHAPEL, WINDSOR

Of all the Hanoverian kings, George III was the most popular, the longest serving and the most tragic. The first George to be born and raised a Briton, and to speak English as his mother tongue, he was the grandson of George II. His father, hated by both parents, had died in 1751 and George was brought up under the strong influence of his mother, a domineering woman, and his tutor Lord Bute, who was also his mother's alleged lover. George was somewhat shy, dull-witted and unenthusiastic about his inheritance, but forced himself to embrace his duties as king, learning by trial and error as much as anything.

The first years of his reign were not so successful. He could not find a Prime Minister that he trusted, and his dour, staid manner did not endear him to his subjects. He was also ridiculed for his typically Hanoverian fleshy features and bulbous eyes, and his injudicious choice of mistresses. It was rumoured that he had secretly married the first of these, a Quakeress from the east end of London, by whom he had three children. By 1770 however he found a reliable minister in Lord North, and had married the beautifully-named but plain-looking Charlotte of Mecklenburg-Strelitz. George's utter faithfulness to his wife from that point on, and the steady stream of children – fifteen in all – became a role model to his people. His steady and reliable manner became a symbol of solid Britishness while France lost its head in revolution and war. George's personal courage was also cheered, when he survived an assassination attempt and when he promised to lead his armies into battle to defeat Napoleon.

The loss of Britain's American colony in 1776 was a huge disappointment, but despite this the country continued the remarkable growth that had started at the beginning of the eighteenth century. George was not the driving force, but he contributed much to the success beyond just being a symbol of strength and patriotism. He patronised art, helping to establish the Royal Academy of Arts. He studied and practised agricultural science so keenly that he became known as 'Farmer George'. He showed a deep interest in military and naval matters, and during his reign the famous victories of Trafalgar and Waterloo were won. A dependable and much-loved king was essential to the maintenance of domestic peace at a time of great social upheaval, as the industrial revolution kicked in and as the values of traditional village life were replaced by the mores of cities and factories.

Towards the end, George's life was increasingly ravaged by sickness and madness. Today these are blamed on a hereditary condition called porphyria, where a chemical imbalance causes both physical and mental deterioration. Doctors of the day were at a loss, prescribing him all manner of cruel and ignorant treatments. The illness followed a pattern of relapse and recovery from about 1788, but the final ten years of his life were spent in almost total isolation in Windsor, abandoned by his family and physicians. Rare moments of lucidity became rarer, interspersed with long periods of agitation, incessant talking and walking. Blind, deaf and dishevelled, our second-longest reigning monarch slipped away almost unnoticed at the age of 82, an unprecedented age for a British king.

George died in Windsor Castle and was buried in St. George's Chapel there, in a break from the traditional Westminster Abbey. There is no grand monument, just a simple inscription 'GR III ROYAL VAULT' on the entrance to his vault on the floor in the centre of the quire, just to the east of Henry VIII's memorial stone.

GEORGE IV 'PRINNY'

♙ BORN 1762
✠ REIGNED FROM 1820 TO 1830
✟ DIED 26 JUNE 1830
AT: WINDSOR CASTLE
BURIED: ST. GEORGE'S CHAPEL, WINDSOR

George IV was a preposterous man – effeminate, overly sensitive, gluttonous and selfish. He was sexually voracious too, moving from one mistress to the next without a care for discretion. Unsurprisingly he incurred the hatred of the conscientious George III, continuing the fractious Hanoverian relationship between father and first-born son that had existed since George I. As Prince of Wales he married a Catholic commoner, the only woman he seems to have had genuine feeling for, breaking both the Royal Marriages Act that stipulated the King's assent for marriage and the Act of Settlement that barred people married to Catholics from the throne. A few years later the marriage was declared annulled and George was forced to marry the rather unhygienic Caroline of Brunswick, as part of an agreement with Parliament to pay his debts. George abandoned Caroline after she gave birth to their daughter Charlotte. She lived abroad, amassing lovers and huge debts, returning only to be locked out of George's coronation at Westminster and to be tried for adultery. Dreadful as she was, George's treatment of her was scandalous and demeaned him further in the public eye. Caroline on the other hand remained hugely popular with the masses.

Today George IV seems a laughable character but in his day he was a serious threat to the establishment. At a time when Britain was threatened by republican France, her people were starved and impoverished by trade restrictions, and new theories of government abounded, many questioned the need for such a profligate and incapable royal. George III's ministers thought deeply before installing him as Prince Regent for the last nine years of his father's illness. Even then 'Prinny' tried to hide in his bedroom, frightened that his new position would thwart his over-indulgences.

As a patron of the arts George did leave a lasting impact on the country. He amassed an impressive collection of paintings. He read the novels of Scott and Austen enthusiastically. And of course his love of architecture led to the construction of Brighton Pavilion, with its fantastic Chinese and Indian themes, and the expansion of Buckingham House into Buckingham Palace. He also rebuilt Windsor Castle, creating sumptuous state rooms that can be visited today. His influence left us with the style we now call Regency, associated strongly with glorious buildings in Bath and Regent's Park, and with sophisticated, high-quality furniture.

George grew inordinately fat, feasting and drinking without consideration for expense or health. Inevitably this contributed to a great deal of illness, and eventually his death from gastric haemorrhage accompanied by cirrhosis of the liver and several other complaints. It is said that crowds thronged to guffaw at his dead body as it lay in state, a sad end for a pathetic monarch.

He died at Windsor Castle and is buried in St. George's Chapel. There is no monument to him.

91. Windsor Castle, seen from the Cambridge Gate on the Long Walk. George died in the semi-state apartment rooms.

WILLIAM IV 'SILLY BILLY'

   BORN 1765
   REIGNED FROM 1830 TO 1837
   DIED 20 JUNE 1837
   AT: WINDSOR CASTLE
   BURIED: ST. GEORGE'S CHAPEL, WINDSOR

At 65, William IV came to the throne a good deal older than the age at which many previous monarchs had died. He was not expected to be king – but neither of his elder brothers had any surviving children, and both predeceased him. The crown was at a very low point, ridiculed as it had been during George IV's reign, and in desperate need of a strong and respectable figure. William wasn't perhaps the ideal person to do this. He was renowned as a somewhat wild man, full of oddities, and with dozens of mistresses against his record. He wasn't the most intelligent of royals, and he had the shadow of his father's madness hanging over him. William was however a man of the people. He had spent his youth as a sailor, rising to captain a frigate, and was never happier than when brawling, drinking or whoring with his rough shipmates. He had a remarkably easy-going manner, to such an extent that he would stroll around London greeting people, shaking their hands and refusing to be deferred to against anybody's wishes. For this, and for his blunt matter-of-fact way of speaking his mind, the people loved him, in spite of his eccentricities.

William was a conscientious king who worked hard to clear the backlog of unsigned papers that his brother George IV had left. His ministers respected him for that, although they had to show extreme patience when explaining affairs to him that he could not understand. William, whilst regretting the fading power of the monarchy, at least recognised the need for reform. Aside from the contempt with which George had been held, there were again dangerous currents of social change threatening to throw Britain into revolution. Prime amongst these was the fact that the new, fast-growing industrial cities were barely represented in Parliament, and power was dictated by a handful of rich landowners. Protests and riots prevailed. William, though not without reservations, encouraged the Reform Act of 1832 to grant votes to a much wider group of men. Another step towards democracy had been taken; another nail had been driven into the executive monarch's coffin.

Despite fathering ten illegitimate children by a previous mistress, William was unable to produce any surviving heirs with his wife Adelaide. Aside from this it was an incredibly happy union. Adelaide tempered much of his more eccentric behaviour, and stood loyally by him. As his health deteriorated, William wished for two things. Firstly to see his niece and heir Victoria reach her eighteenth birthday, ensuring that her mother, whom William hated, would never have control as regent. Secondly to live to see one final 'Waterloo Day', the 18 June celebration of Wellington's greatest victory. Both of these he achieved, dying at Windsor Castle on 20 June surrounded by his illegitimate children and his grandchildren. He was much mourned. Though known as 'Silly Billy' for his often embarrassing antics, he was a people's king who had done much to restore popular faith in the crown. William was buried in St. George's Chapel but there is no memorial to him.

VICTORIA

   ⌂   BORN 1819
   ✠   REIGNED FROM 1837 TO 1901
   ♰   DIED 22 JANUARY 1901
         AT: OSBORNE HOUSE, ISLE OF WIGHT
         BURIED: FROGMORE, WINDSOR

In many ways Victoria is our most remarkable monarch. She gave her name to perhaps the most exciting epoch in Britain's history. She presided over the building of railways, the invention of the telephone, and the creation of the largest empire ever seen. Stupendous wealth and abject poverty sat side by side in great, industrialised cities. By the end of her reign almost every country in Europe was ruled by one of her descendants, through judicious marriages. Jenner and Lister were at the forefront of a revolution in medicine. Faraway wars such as the Crimean and Boer were photographed for daily newspapers, troops were tended by a new type of nurse inspired by Seacole and Nightingale. Britain became the hub of the trading world, with great red-brick buildings proclaiming the Victorians' financial and architectural greatness. Yet what of the woman herself, Queen of a United Kingdom, Empress of India?

In many respects she was quite ordinary, highly conservative and very dependent on father-figures. Born Alexandrina Victoria, and known as Drina in her youth, she had a strict upbringing with no father, a distant mother and few companions. She was the only surviving grandchild of George III, through his fourth son Edward, as both George IV and William IV failed to produce heirs. She acceded to the throne at the age of eighteen knowing little of the ways of the world, but harbouring a steely resolve not to be beaten, and to do her duty. Her first speech in the House of Lords took everyone by surprise. Calm, perceptive and mature, she belied her youth. With the expert guidance of her first Prime Minister Lord Melbourne she gained the respect of Whigs and Tories alike. She had limited powers, but she held much influence.

Mistakes were made that soon dinted her popularity. Albert's arrival as Prince Consort quickly put her back on track. He was intelligent, interested in the welfare of the poor, devoted to the furtherment of science, an enthusiastic supporter of trade, and best of all, totally devoted to Victoria. They worked side by side, produced nine children and made a famously happy partnership – one that Victoria contrived to damage towards the end with her intemperate arguments. When Albert died Victoria was distraught. She wore black for the rest of her life and retreated into seclusion, often at Osborne House on the Isle of Wight or at Balmoral in the Highlands. Many people grew critical of her lack of involvement in public life, demanding an end to the monarchy, or abdication in favour of the son she disliked the most, Prince Edward.

Victoria weathered all these storms, and as she passed through her fiftieth and sixtieth jubilees, became hugely popular once more. She was the symbol of Britain's success, the heart of the vast empire, the pillar of cherished traditions. Most of her subjects had known no other monarch. She was in general a healthy person, though grown very fat and short (several inches shorter than her five feet two inches at marriage) and was spared a lingering death. She succumbed to heart failure at her favourite retreat of Osborne House, surrounded by many children and grandchildren, supported on either side by the future Edward VII and Kaiser Wilhelm.

Osborne House is today managed by English Heritage, who have maintained many features as they would have been in Victoria's day. The setting is beautiful, with far views over the Solent to Portsmouth, and you can certainly understand why it became the queen's favourite residence. Victoria died in the Queen's Bedroom where you can see the plaque installed by her children in her memory.

Such was her love of Albert and of privacy that she did not want to be buried in St. George's Chapel or Westminster Abbey, but at the mausoleum she had built in the grounds of Frogmore House, another favourite retreat, in Windsor. Inside the mausoleum are beautiful marble effigies of the Queen and her Consort, capturing their faces at the time of Albert's death. Victoria is therefore a much younger, slimmer figure than the fat, old lady dressed in black that we mostly think of today. The mausoleum itself is a remarkable, octagonal construction with a beautiful Victorian interior of the highest order.

92. Osborne House viewed from below the terraced gardens.

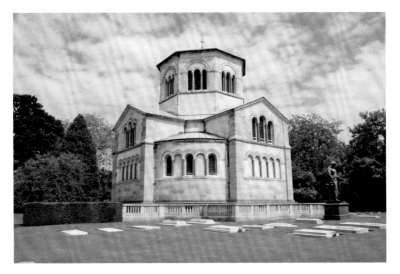

93. Victoria's mausoleum at Frogmore. The tombstones are of various royals, including Edward VIII, beyond the far right of this photo.

EDWARD VII 'BERTIE'

⚱ BORN 1841

✠ REIGNED FROM 1901 TO 1910

✟ DIED 6 MAY 1910

AT: BUCKINGHAM PALACE, LONDON

BURIED: ST. GEORGE'S CHAPEL, WINDSOR

The Edwardian era was a golden time in British history. The wealthy basked in the glow of the riches generated by their predecessors, indulging in unprecedented luxuries. The motor car brought faster travel to new destinations, huge liners brought opulence to cross-Atlantic cruises. Strict Victorian principles of hard work surrendered to a love of pleasure, led most distinctly and enthusiastically by the new king, Edward VII. The stuffy, reclusive old queen and the nineteenth century made way for the hedonistic, clubbable king and the glittering promise of the twentieth century. New styles of clothing, music, film, architecture – all seemed to herald the changing of the old guard, in a peaceful Britain untouched as yet by war on its doorstep.

Edward VII, known invariably as 'Bertie', played his part admirably in the transformation. He was the eldest son of Victoria and Albert, and was their everlasting despair. Albert, who was otherwise a paragon of virtue, intelligence and right-mindedness, believed that his son should be brought up to be a 'good' king. This meant endless lessons, rigid rules and little time for fun. Edward rebelled. He was a poor student, threw things at his teachers and played tricks on his siblings. The well-meaning Albert had failed to understand his son's character, and like all the Hanoverians before, a gulf developed between them. Edward's early initiation into sexual scandal, with Nellie Clifden during an army training camp in Ireland, was a contributory factor to Albert's early death, and Victoria never forgave him for it. Edward was shunned, considered unfit to be a future king and barred from access to State papers until he was in his fifties.

What Edward lacked in tact and statesmanship he more than made up with charisma. People were charmed by him, as well as fascinated by his continual affairs with numerous women and his vices of gambling, drinking and over-eating. His marriage to the beautiful Alexandra of Denmark was surprisingly successful despite his constant infidelities. Edward acceded to the throne at the very late age of 59, and, whilst still very much a pleasure-seeker, attended to his duties conscientiously. He enjoyed diplomacy, helping to forge good relations with other European countries and in particular France. During his reign the two countries formulated the Entente Cordiale. At home his affable nature was far more popular than his mother's sour-faced reserve, and his country loved him for it. His reign may have been short – only nine years – but it was so successful it lent its name to a period that even now is looked back on with much nostalgia.

Edward died at Buckingham Palace of a heart attack from complications brought about by bronchitis, made worse by his smoking habit. He was mourned sincerely, and his funeral was attended by many thousands.

He was buried in St. George's Chapel, originally under the Albert Memorial Chapel but then moved to the south side of the high altar after Alexandra died. The white marble effigies are quite beautiful but difficult to inspect closely as they are high up. The location is perhaps one of the best of all our monarchs' tombs, opposite Edward IV's glorious chantry, next to Henry VI's tomb, overlooked by the high altar and diffused in light from the stained glass windows behind. At the king's feet lies his favourite dog 'Caesar'.

94. Buckingham Palace.

95. Edward's and Alexandra's tomb effigies, viewed from above.

GEORGE V 'THE SAILOR KING'

🕮 BORN 1865

✠ REIGNED FROM 1910 TO 1936

✝ DIED 20 JANUARY 1936

  AT: SANDRINGHAM HOUSE, NORFOLK

  BURIED: ST. GEORGE'S CHAPEL, WINDSOR

George V had the unhappy responsibility of reigning throughout the First World War, an exceptionally trying time for the country and for the king himself. Being of German descent, with a German surname (Saxe-Coburg-Gotha) and with many German relatives, including his cousin Kaiser Wilhelm, he worried about public hostility and struggled with his own personal conflict between patriotic duty and family loyalty. European kings were overthrown during the war as part of a massive social upheaval – the Romanovs in Russia, the Hohenzollerns in Germany – and George had just cause for anxiety about his own position. Britain avoided revolution, but George's reign saw radical events such as women's suffrage, independence in Ireland, the great General Strike of 1926 and the first Labour Government under Ramsay MacDonald. These were torrid times for the generally introspective, conservative George.

George was the second son of Edward VII. To the relief of many, George's older brother Prince Albert Victor, or 'Eddy', dissipated, slow-witted and of doubtful sexual morality, died in 1892. At the time George was enjoying life as a naval officer, but upon becoming heir to his father, returned to England to lead a more sheltered existence, hunting and walking at his Sandringham estate. Here he set up home with his dead brother's fiancée Mary or May of Teck and for the next seventeen years honed his shooting skills, raised his family with an overly-strict bearing, and developed one of the country's finest stamp collections. He never lost his bluff sailor ways, shouting at people and preferring a simple cottage on the estate rather than the spacious Sandringham House itself. His marriage was a particularly successful one, the two being quietly devoted to one another.

After accession, George did his best to do his duty. During the war he visited the soldiers near the front line on several occasions, once being thrown from his horse by the men's hearty cheering and suffering a broken pelvis. He changed his family name from the German Saxe-Coburg-Gotha to the endearingly English Windsor. He suffered his ministers, despite his personal misgivings about their politics, and they in turn found him a pleasant though dull and simple man to deal with. The loss of southern Ireland hit George badly, as he had worked hard to broker a compromise. His relationship with his eldest son 'David', later Edward VIII, followed the all-too-familiar Hanoverian tradition of contempt bordering on hatred. David was a dissolute youth who rankled with his father's strict sense of propriety and duty. Indeed George's strict treatment of all his children is perhaps the greatest criticism that can be levelled at him, for otherwise he proved to be a congenial monarch in an exceedingly difficult period.

Illness dogged George in his final years. Enforced convalescence from septicaemia on the south coast of England brought about the infamous quotation "Bugger Bognor!" At the age of 70 George succumbed to a bronchial infection, and died at his beloved Sandringham House. Many years later it was discovered that his doctor had hastened his death with morphia and cocaine so that the event would be published in *The Times* and not in the lesser papers that came out later in the day.

Sandringham House is the current Queen's personal possession, but is open to the public during the summer. It is a peaceful, welcoming place, airy and light, far removed from the noise and pressures of London. There are many guns, photos, stuffed creatures and specially adapted hunting carriages on display to remind you of one of royalty's principal pleasures in this part of Norfolk.

George was buried in St. George's Chapel in Windsor. A magnificent tomb designed by Lutyens, with white stone effigies of the King and Queen, was raised some three years later in the north aisle of the nave. It is perhaps one of our most beautiful effigies, startlingly white with sleeping angels caressing their crowns and a lion and unicorn at their feet.

96. The west front of Sandringham House, Norfolk.

97. George V's tomb in St. George's Chapel, Windsor.

98. The position of George V's tomb in the north aisle.

EDWARD VIII

- ☖ BORN 1894
- ✠ REIGNED FROM JANUARY 1936 TO DECEMBER 1936
- ♱ DIED 28 MAY 1972
- AT: BOIS DE BOULOGNE, PARIS, FRANCE
- BURIED: FROGMORE, WINDSOR

To his adoring public Edward Albert Christian George Andrew Patrick David had an enviable, perfect existence. Handsome, rich, personable and heir to the throne, as a prince he acquired the sort of status normally reserved for film stars. He circulated in the highest of society, undertook foreign state visits on behalf of his father, was a decorated officer in the First World War and had affairs with a succession of married women. He also showed concern for the impoverished, particularly areas of South Wales hit hardest by the 1930s depression. He was a breath of fresh air to the stuffy monarchy, still beholden to Victorian virtues and Tory values. The people loved him, but they were worshiping his exterior persona and knew little of the man himself.

For David, as he was known to his family, was frustrated and insecure. He desperately sought love, approval and control from his women, having received precious little affection from his mother Mary. From adolescence he found it nigh impossible to form close bonds with any of his family or friends, growing detached even from his beloved younger brother Bertie (later George VI). He couldn't concentrate on important matters, preferring easy pleasure to hard work, but quickly became bored even with his luxurious lifestyle. Following the Hanoverian tradition, David fell out with his father, who disagreed with his fast, loose lifestyle, and who was worried about the impact of David's affairs on the monarchy. George V predicted that after his death David would "ruin himself in twelve months". And he was right.

Acceding to the throne in January 1936 as Edward VIII, he proceeded to irritate his ministers by ignoring paperwork and official duties, and by continuing to pursue his playboy lifestyle. Worse still he maintained his infatuation with the married and once-divorced Wallis Warfield Simpson. The Government decided that marriage to an American divorcee, whilst not unconstitutional, would be bad for the country. After months of seeking a compromise, Edward decided that his only option was to abdicate in favour of his brother Bertie. In his abdication speech he said "I have found it impossible to carry the heavy burden of responsibility and to discharge my duties as King as I would wish to do without the help and support of the woman I love".

At the time it caused a furore, and greatly upset his British subjects. Even by exiling himself in France however Edward still managed to court controversy. He met and saluted Hitler, and was accused of supporting fascism. He was even believed to have helped the Germans with their invasion plans for Belgium. Winston Churchill appointed him as Governor of the Bahamas for the duration of the Second World War, as the place where he was least likely to harm the war effort. Afterwards he and Wallis returned to Paris, as Duke and Duchess of Windsor, to live out their rather futile lives as minor celebrities. There were meetings with members of the royal family, most notably with Elizabeth II just weeks before Edward's death in 1972, and occasional returns to Britain for funerals, but little in the manner of a full reconciliation.

Edward died of throat cancer at 4 Rue du Champ d'Entrainement in the Bois de Boulogne in Paris. The house is easy enough to find, but not at all easy to see, being in private hands and behind a substantial gate and fence.

His body was brought back to Windsor and buried in the grounds of Frogmore House beside Victoria's mausoleum. The Duchess was buried next to him 14 years later. Their tombstones are simple, in keeping with the other royals buried there, and although you cannot approach them closely, you can get a decent view from the gate behind them. Frogmore is open only a few days each year, but is well worth a visit for a more intimate view of royal life compared to the nearby Windsor Castle.

99. The gate to the house in the Bois de Boulogne lent to Edward by the City of Paris upon his return from the Bahamas after 1945.

100. Edward's and Wallis's tombstones in Frogmore. Edward's is the furthermost in this photo.

GEORGE VI

⚜ BORN 1895

✠ REIGNED FROM 1936 TO 1952

✟ DIED 6 FEBRUARY 1952

    AT: SANDRINGHAM HOUSE, NORFOLK

    BURIED: ST. GEORGE'S CHAPEL, WINDSOR

George VI (known as Bertie) lived in the shadow of his handsome, outgoing brother Edward VIII (known as David) for so long. The shadow was all the more exaggerated because of George's debilitating stammer, his knock-knees and gastric upsets when young, and his academic failings. Like his brother he was deprived of maternal affection, and grew into an unassuming young man with low self-esteem. He found outlets for his frustrations in sports, in hunting and eventually in the Royal Navy, where, although by no means brilliant, he found a life with which he was comfortable. He took part in the Battle of Jutland in the First World War, an experience he was lucky to survive, and one of which he was justifiably proud.

Where Edward was a shining star who faded into a non-entity as he grew older, George was the exact opposite. Bit by bit he overcame his weaknesses and grew into a superlative monarch, not through heroic leadership, but through solid devotion to his duty. There were several reasons behind his transformation. His judicious marriage to Elizabeth Bowes-Lyon (the late Queen Mother) provided a loving, cheerful and hugely supportive counterpart. Years of hard graft with a speech tutor helped him overcome the worst of his stammer, and calm his nerves in front of an audience. The abdication of his brother forced him, unwillingly, to take on the responsibilities of king, and this became a turning point in his personality. His dogged sense of duty and devotion to the institution of the monarchy meant he couldn't run away like his brother had, so he faced his challenges squarely and took inspiration from them.

Most of all it was his behaviour during the Second World War that was a watershed for George. He refused to flee London while it was being bombed by the Germans, although it would have been perfectly acceptable to do so. Instead he and the queen visited the dispossessed and stricken families of London daily to give them their support, to show that neither Britain nor the royal family would bow to foreign incursion. George became a hero to the people, beloved as a symbol of courage and hope. After the war George further earned the respect of his ministers, as he oversaw another period of massive social change characterised by economic hardship, not always understanding Government policy but always supporting and helping.

Throughout his adult life George had been a heavy smoker, and inevitably it was this that did for him, though the connection between smoking and cancer was not fully understood. Upon hearing of his death, London traffic came to a standstill as people stood, wept and mourned a king who they felt had truly been one of them. His makes a remarkable story of transformation, and of success achieved, not through the aggressive absolutism of his distant predecessor William I, but through determination, decency and hard work.

George died at Sandringham House, just a few days after waving his daughter, the future Elizabeth II, off to a visit to Africa. He is buried in a specially built memorial chapel on the north side of St. George's Chapel, Windsor. Inside there are bronze medallions of the king and queen, and a simple black stone bearing the inscription of their names.

101. The entrance to the George VI memorial chapel. The memorial slab is on the floor; there are various other memorials to both George and his wife, the late Queen Mother, inside the chapel.

Sources of photographs

Geoff Brown: 1, 2, 3, 4, 5, 9, 10 ,11, 12, 13, 14, 15, 16, 17, 18, 19, 20, 21, 22, 23, 24, 25, 26, 30, 31, 32, 33, 34, 35, 37, 38, 39, 41, 42, 44, 45, 47, 49, 50, 51, 53, 54, 55, 56, 57, 59, 61, 62, 63, 64, 65, 66, 67, 69, 70, 72, 73, 74, 75, 76, 77, 78, 80, 81, 82, 83, 84, 85, 86, 87, 88, 89, 90, 91, 92, 93, 94, 96, 99, 100

Geoff Brown, with kind permission of the Dean and Canons of Windsor: 46, 48, 71, 98, 101

Geoff Brown, with kind permission of the Dean and Chapter, Canterbury: 40

Geoff Brown, with kind permission of the Chapter of Winchester: 6, 7, 8

Geoff Brown, with kind permission of the Dean and Chapter, Worcester: 27, 28

Copyright Dean and Canons of Windsor: 60, 95, 97

Copyright Dean and Chapter of Westminster: 29, 36, 43, 52, 58, 68, 79

Further reading

The following excellent books and websites are recommended for those wanting either to explore our kings and queens more generally, or study royal deaths and tombs specifically. There are many other books available on individual monarchs, royal houses and periods of history:

Brewer, Clifford, T.D., F.R.C.S., *The Death of Kings*, Abson Books, 2000

Dodson, Aidan, *The Royal Tombs of Great Britain*, Duckworth, 2004

Duffy, Mark, *Royal Tombs of Medieval England*, Tempus, 2003

Erickson, Carolly, *Brief Lives of the English Monarchs*, Constable & Robinson, 2003

Hilliam, David, *Kings, Queens, Bones & Bastards*, Sutton, 1998

Lee, Christopher, *This Sceptred Isle*, BBC & Penguin, 1997

Schama, Simon, *A History of Britain*, BBC Worldwide, 2000

Steane, John, *The Archaeology of the Medieval English Monarchy*, Routledge, 1999

www.englishmonarchs.co.uk
www.royalist.info
www.wikipedia.org